Institutions, Consultants and Transformation

Institutions, Consultants and Transformation

Case Studies from the Development Sector

Edited by

LALITHA IYER

SHAIBAL GUHAROY

First published in 2009 by

Response Books
Business books from SAGE
B1/I-1 Mohan Cooperative Industrial Area
Mathura Road, New Delhi 110 044, India

SAGE Publications Inc
2455 Teller Road
Thousand Oaks, California 91320, USA

SAGE Publications Ltd
1 Oliver's Yard, 55 City Road
London EC1Y 1SP, United Kingdom

SAGE Publications Asia-Pacific Pte Ltd
33 Pekin Street
#02-01 Far East Square
Singapore 048763

Published by Vivek Mehra for SAGE Publications India Pvt. Ltd., typeset in 10.5/12.5 pt Baskerville BE Regular by Star Compugraphics Private Limited, Delhi and printed at Chaman Enterprises, New Delhi.

Library of Congress Cataloging-in-Publication Data Available

ISBN: 978-81-7829-867-2 (Pb)

The SAGE Team: Sugata Ghosh, P.K. Jayanthan and Trinankur Banerjee

||Om Saha nāv avatu
Saha nau bhunaktu
Saha vīryam karavāvahai
Tejasvi nāv adhītam astu
Mā vidvishāvahai||

||Let us together be protected
Let us together be nourished by God's blessings
Let us together join our mental forces in strength
for the benefit of humanity
Let our efforts at learning be luminous and filled with joy
and endowed with the force of purpose
Let us never be poisoned with the seeds of hatred for anyone.||

Contents

List of Tables viii
List of Figures ix
List of Boxes x
Foreword by Rolf P. Lynton xi
Acknowledgements xvii

1. Organisational Change and Institution Building in the Social Sector–Some Reflections 1
Lalitha Iyer

2. C-POD II 18
Shaibal Guharoy

3. Case I–Ekta: Swimming with the Tide 22

4. Case II–Chaturya: An Experiment in Collective Leadership 60

5. Case III–Prakruti: Gender Mainstreaming and Organisational Development 85

6. Case IV–Triveni: A Journey of Inclusion 114

7. Case V–Panchim: A Story of Renewal 145

8. Techniques in Intervention and Design 187
Lalitha Iyer

About the Editors and Contributors 205
Index 211

List of Tables

3.1 Analysis of Tools and Techniques–Ekta 53

4.1 Analysis of Tools and Techniques–Chaturya 79

5.1 Analysis of Tools and Techniques–Prakruti 109

6.1 Analysis of Tools and Techniques–Triveni 140

7.1 Tools and Techniques used in Workshops–Panchim 157
7.2 Analysis of Tools and Techniques–Panchim 179
7.3 Change Agent Orientation Workshop 181
7.4 Skill-building Workshop 1–Panchim 182
7.5 Skill-building Workshop 2–Panchim 182
7.6 Skill-building Workshop 3–Panchim 183

8.1 Elements of Institutional Capacity 195

List of Figures

1.1	Stages of an OD Process	2
3.1	The Organisational Structure of Ekta	25
3.2	The Intervention Cycle for Ekta	28
4.1	Organisational Structure of Chaturya	62
4.2	Steps in Collective Leadership Intervention	63
5.1	The Changes Required–Inner and Outer	90
6.1	Organisational Structure of Triveni	117
6.2	The Intervention Cycle for Triveni	118
7.1	Stakeholders in the Panchim OD Process	148
7.2	The Intervention Cycle for Panchim	149
7.3	Organisational Structure of Panchim	150

List of Boxes

3.1	A Scientific Orientation	38
3.2	Views of Dr Ram	46
5.1	Accompaniment Process	93
6.1	The Shared Vision	121
6.2	Projects Identified by CMG	123
7.1	The Survey Results	155
7.2	P-4 Groups	159
7.3	Financial Inclusions	177
8.1	Johari Window–*avatars*	191

Foreword

On four very important grounds I welcome this set of five case studies of organisation development (OD) consulting in social, non-governmental organisations (NGOs): the work is in an important but long-neglected domain; the seasoned practitioners themselves have recorded and written about it, so these accounts are first-hand and from the field; any funding was in-country; and the institutional mechanism to collect, shape and issue them continues.

First, I will tell briefly why these are so important. And then, I will also go on to indicate three directions in which work for the same purposes may be enhanced and become more widely established.

OD Consulting in NGOs

OD consulting with NGOs has had only a recent and ragged start: consulting with an NGO as a whole and on the NGO's own inside agenda. For other services–helping install new technical services such as IT and most commonly to ensure quality accounting to satisfy auditors, funders and regulatory agencies, all of them outsiders–consultants have featured prominently.

Now, with globalisation, the rapid growth of OD consulting in the corporate sector is spilling over to NGOs. Most studies here reflect this parentage, but uneasily, as if

NGOs were stepchildren needing to catch up against odds. So consulting with NGOs also commands far lower fees; consequently, consultants, as several authors of these studies have done, tend to mix the NGOs with commercial work. Copying corporate OD approaches and methods is then a ready temptation, but a very limiting and hazardous one.

By their very nature NGOs have to be wide-open systems; they espouse larger values and relate to their worlds differently from corporations. Contextual understanding and collaborative working with autonomous partners are the lifeblood of effective NGOs. Helping to incorporate these aspects into the internal workings of an NGO constitutes the key task of effective consulting with NGOs. So learning between the sectors is welcome, but circumspectly, with caution. I will return to the difference and refer to the framework I use to ensure that my attention and consulting is broad enough for work with such open systems.

In fact, very important learning should soon flow the other way. New technologies, ever more diverse workforces and highly mobile professionals in multicultural locations strongly favour opening up of traditionally closed systems and ensuring that both individuals and sub-systems are assured of high autonomy. NGOs have much experience on these dimensions, and consultants working with them can document and refine it for wider sharing.

First-hand Accounts by the Consultants Themselves

The first-hand accounts here are a refreshing return to basics; they offer opportunity for peers to discuss challenging situations they face in the way physicians routinely confer with colleagues over challenging, difficult cases. Ideally they would display organisational life 'in three dimensions and real time'. These fall short of that–and I will return to practical possibilities of getting closer–but in telling the stories themselves, practitioners do essentially better than researchers could do, even the best, for researchers must remain outsiders and have to reconstruct the events anew.

And it is not only the first-hand descriptions that can be the richest. Uniquely important is that only the practitioners themselves identify what they bring by way of assumptions and earlier experiences to understanding and helping the people and situations in this particular NGO, on this day. In short, only they can unscramble (as best as they can) their personal projections from 'the world out there' that they mean the reader too to see truly. One study here (Ekta) does this explicitly and well.

In-country Funding

In-country funding underscores the importance of the work and goes further than foreign agencies can, to signal its high relevance, timeliness and essential continuity. Long, deep-rooted familiarity with local conditions and needs make this type of financial backing especially valuable.

An Institutional Mechanism for Continuing this Work

All the consulting presented in these studies preceded the recording and organising them into this body of work. Their publication now may surface others as good. This too would be worth collecting, shaping with colleagues, and publishing.

For that stimulation, encouragement, collegiate support and technical services clearly requires a minimal infrastructure; spasmodic, scattered personal efforts of individual consultants are simply not enough. That same, simple mechanism, could branch out to include a deliberate, orderly programme for expanding the field of consulting with NGOs and increasing the number of professionals competent to do it.

And so to the future, I envisage four immediately possible steps ahead.

From Organisation Development (OD) to Institution Development (ID)

The most incisive step forward could be distinguishing NGOs from organisations with a narrower focus, and identifying the consulting appropriate for each. In contrast to corporate purposes, NGOs have 'changing their environment' as their core aim, be it multiplying new livelihoods in the area, empowering women, ensuring equitable justice for all sections, raising educational standards, protecting the forest or ensuring clean water for all.

Developmental aims like these require that NGOs behave with much greater openness with the communities around them and that effective engagements with them be mutual, as indeed befits totally autonomous partners. These essential distinctive features make organising and managing NGOs extra complex.

To mark this difference, from more closed systems, it is better to identify NGOs as *institutions* along with schools and public services work towards uplifting people and their environment as their reason for existing.

Happily, these extra complexities can be mapped and managed systematically. International work on institution-building has identified five 'internal components' and six 'external linkages' as essential to keep continuously in view and interrelated. The internal components are mission, leadership, resources, programmes and structure, and the external linkages, enabling, functional, normative, diffuse, collegial and supportive. This, or a similarly well-researched schema, can help consultants make sure to cover all essential bases in their work with NGOs and in presenting their findings and learning.

Providing Extra Needed Supports

With changing the environment as their very purpose, NGOs set themselves up to encounter opposition and swim continually against the stream. Further developments and unfamiliar ways will only continue to raise doubts and indecision in the community. Early institution-building studies underestimated the extra supports NGOs need to cope with the counter-currents.

In the beginning collegiate linkages were added to the list of essentials, followed by more institutional support and most recently, individual and personal support as well. All reflect how tough it usually is to initiate and sustain significant changes community-wide, and yet more to keep doing it as a career.

Certainly, provision of adequate institutional and also personal support should figure prominently in all consultants' recommendations and reports.

Joint Reporting of Consultants with Client

With collaboration being the essential mode and method of consulting with NGOs, it would 'walk the talk' most convincingly, to make the reporting and publishing of it, mutual and shared. That additional step, openly taken, would further reinforce the basic values of this work and publish them further.

From Few to Many

Consultants to work with NGOs, now pitifully few, could increase reliably and quickly if each current consultant used all possible opportunities to team up with an understudy intent on gaining consulting knowledge with an experienced practitioner. In face-to-face contacts with client(s), the consultant could gain from the extra pair of eyes and ears and enrich understanding from discussions afterwards off-site. The understudy could also have the special task of recording and documenting more fully the consultation as it proceeds, and then, also provide better ongoing data for its reporting.

Above all, this would strengthen the profession most reliably and quickly with people experienced in the field.

Rolf P. Lynton
North Carolina

Acknowledgements

It was our good fortune that we had the opportunity to coordinate this endeavour. Many individuals and institutions have supported this work and nurtured us along this path. We take this moment to gratefully acknowledge all the support.

It has been a fascinating process to gather the material on these case studies. Contributors have taken the risk of sharing the dilemmas and the difficulties they faced–the behind-the-scenes angst that is so real, yet rarely recorded in full detail.

It is a deeper level of practising the professional values of change facilitation. It is an effort to reach out to those wishing to tread this path, a road much travelled but yet less known. We thank the contributors for 'telling it like it is', and look forward to learning more along with them and many others who will be inspired by them. The reviewers too have played a crucial role capturing the elements that got institutionalised through these change initiatives.

The organisations which were the host sites for these experiences have been very generous in their support too. In the interest of honouring their privacy we hold back from acknowledging them individually by name. Together they represent some of the most respected institutions in the social development space.

Rolf Lynton and Ronken Lynton brought in their special expertise in building an emotional sanctuary for the contributors and the reviewers to work together to get the focus clear. Their very pragmatic suggestions and support was the much needed element to help us pull it all together.

Our special thanks are due to Dr U. Balaji of Satyam Foundation for recognising the need for such work and taking up this project. Satyam Technology Centre was a quiet retreat for the contributors and reviewers to wrestle with the rewrites.

Our colleagues at ThinkSoft Consultants have been an unfailing source of inspiration and support. In particular, we acknowledge the support and encouragement from M. Sashikumar and K. Lalita, and the hard work put in by Snigdha Vasireddy and Sarayu Kalyani.

Much of the material developed was 'tested' on the participants in the Organisational Change Facilitation Programme (OCFP) conducted by the Human and Institutional Development Forum (HIDF) in Bangalore. Their feedback and suggestions proved crucial too.

Sir Ratan Tata Trust has provided the financial support under their Roopantaran Initiative to make this project possible. We are particularly grateful to Arun Pandhi, Vartika Jaini and Mukesh Tiwary for the crucial role they played in shaping the project.

We have much hope that the process begun will continue to spread in different forms and shapes. We know that there are many inadequacies and own full responsibility for them. We invite feedback, suggestions and support. And if this spurs some others to do a better job of it all, we would be the happiest.

Lalitha Iyer
Shaibal Guharoy
Mamta Upudi
(The C-POD Team)

1

Organisational Change and Institution Building in the Social Sector—Some Reflections

LALITHA IYER

BACKGROUND

The development sector in India is going through a process of expansion and diversification. NGOs, Civil Society Organisations, Community-Based Organisations and large projects within the government systems are engaged in development activities. 'Corporate Social Responsibility' has created a new breed of corporatised NGOs with their own work culture. Many observers see the need for well-grounded organisation development (OD) practices as the sector matures and consolidates itself.

Issues of complexity and scale demand that the organisations are themselves well configured and handle their internal dynamics effectively before attempting to change the world. OD work in the development sector has therefore become very interesting and challenging.

In this scenario, OD practitioners specially engaged with development organisations were invited to share their experiences and collectively reflect on their work and its relevance for the sector. The C-POD (Community of Practitioners in Organisation Development) conference was organised with these objectives at Hyderabad during 14 and 15 November 2005.

Leaders of NGOs and academics were also invited to share their perspectives.

OD practitioners specifically shared their experiences at the different stages of an OD process (Figure 1.1).

Figure 1.1 Stages of an OD Process

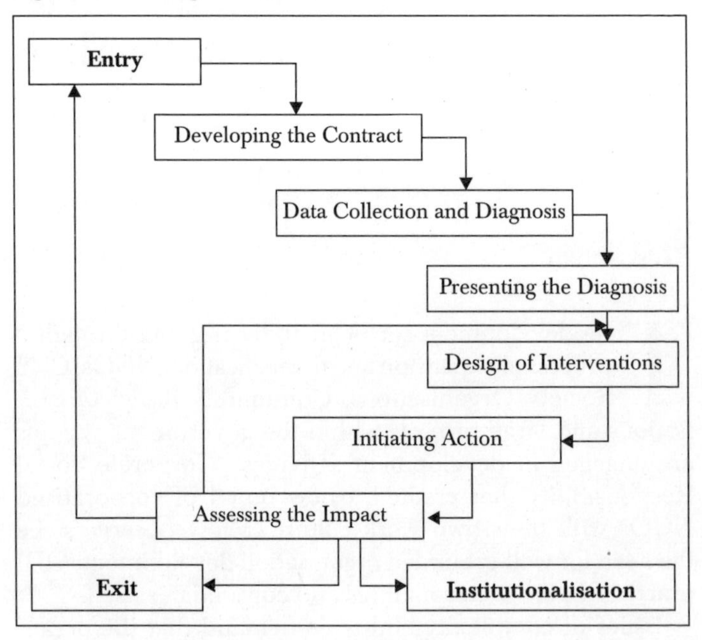

First Contact

The first contact was usually made by the client organisation on the basis of the profile of or previous work done by the consultant. Sometimes it was at the behest of a funding organisation.

Entry point had also been through some human resources (HR) or training intervention, which builds some confidence and relationship between the consultant and client organisation. In one case it was a gender-mainstreaming project that became an OD intervention eventually. Personal contacts, relationships, past records, labels, and recommendations were seen as important.

Practitioners also discussed how they chose projects; the work of the organisation–the intuitive feel during initial conversations were all considered important. Some of them felt a special sense of excitement and energy in working with the development sector clients because of their respect for the social impact and relevance of these organisations.

Terms of Reference or Consultancy Task Definition

Clarifying the scope of work and defining the stages or steps and outputs at various stages invariably took longer than expected. However, it was important to take this time.

Some crucial aspects got clarified in this process.

It became clear who the 'principal client' was. For the consultant, clarity about the level of backing as well as the doubts in the minds of various significant individuals or groups in the organisation became visible at this stage. Sometimes the CEO would be the change champion, sometimes the board or governing body. The top management commitment to the process was also built up at this stage. Similarly, the misgivings, doubts and anxieties about an OD process within the organisation were addressed. When the terms of reference were clear, the distinction between the OD consultant's role and that of other advisors and experts providing inputs was understood and accepted. The consultant had clarity about the legitimate authority figure he or she could rely on in case of difficulties.

In some cases, the exit was planned and accepted. In others, the role continued and evolved, as the organisation moved ahead. The tasks of the consultant were redefined each time, even though the consultant did not change.

When the consultancy is provided by an NGO with mandate for OD work, the process takes the tone of a partnership and the outcomes become very important for the consultant. Terms like accompaniment or partnering are used to describe such engagements. The difference of being in 'development' (perspectives of pro-poor/participatory/gender and diversity sensitive/rights based, and so on) influences the way the consultant plays the role. The OD process becomes one more way of institutionalising these values and beliefs or mission. Some consultants prefer to move into the role of advisors. Sometimes, they accept positions in the governance of the organisation. The importance of defining and holding these boundaries was discussed at length.

Themes for the Interventions

Some of the recurring themes for the interventions were:

- Strengthening of the middle management.
- Building collective leadership.
- Ensuring gender mainstreaming.
- Reducing dependence on the founder or a single major authority figure.
- Checking the viability and sustainability of the organisation.
- Ensuring smooth transition from small to medium or large scale operations.
- Looking into issues of scaling up.

Data Collection

It is important to work as close to the ground as possible and understand the core tasks of the client. Presenting data about the situation to the insiders, in such a way that they build their own strategy, was found to be useful.

Anxieties about the situation and resistance to change across the organisation had to be handled during these stages. Discussions with individual staff members sometimes became very intense and emotional; the consultant had to use counselling techniques. There were several examples of constituting an internal change management group to take care of these legitimate concerns and work continuously for the changes identified.

Some of the approaches that were briefly mentioned were Large Scale Interactive Processes, Appreciative Enquiry and Future Search conferences. These methodologies were very useful in bringing the whole organisation into the change process and involving a variety of stakeholders.

Practitioners also referred to the tools they used for climate surveys, assessment of internal factors like motivation, gender sensitivity, individual interviews, moderation methods and other visualisation tools.

Diagnosis and Design of Interventions

Confronting the organisation with the data to get them to accept the picture presented by the diagnosis was the biggest challenge. The principal client sometimes found it hard to accept the data presented. The change process could unfold only when there was acceptance of at least some elements of the diagnosis and the generation of some acceptable hypotheses.

One continuous thread was the emphasis on involving the entire organisation in the diagnosing process itself. A participative diagnosis generated a participative process for change. It also developed the resilience of the organisation in the longer run. In a multi-layered setting, the organisation level diagnosis process closely mirrored that at the branch level.

The data was presented either to the whole organisation or a cross section, both for cross checking and for helping the group to deal with its anxieties.

The consultants facilitated the co-creation of hypotheses. This usually involved exploration of self-level, interpersonal and organisational processes.

Some specific themes that emerged in different interventions were:

- Perspective building on gender.
- Skill building for women staff members.
- Emphasising the 'sustainability' element in NGO work.
- Emphasising development orientation in mainstream institutions.

Initiating Action

Action would flow only when there was sufficient commitment at the top management level. Some of the ways which proved useful in facilitating action were:

- Setting up of an internal core group.
- Developing a parallel structure for internal consultancy and interacting with external consultants.

- Developing the capacities of a group of internal change agents.
- Evolving processes to provide opportunity to share and reflect experiences of the changes in progress to foster collaboration.
- Periodic review and monitoring of the progress in the implementation steps.

Evolving criteria for forming the core group and building in all shades of opinion within the core group were both very important. The spirit of the change theme had to touch the frontline of the organisation. The consultant had to find ways to reach out to the individuals at all levels in the organisation.

Accompaniment visits by the consultant at regular intervals were found to be useful. The growing trust between the principal client, the staff members and the consultants was an indicator of the exercise progressing positively.

Completion of Programme and Exit

Some consultants emphasised the need to define their exit at the time of building the contract itself. It was important to bring about a comfortable closure of the process. An undefined lingering could sometimes be an indication of dependency.

There were some exits that the consultants were unprepared for. Sometimes the exit seemed to happen naturally. In one instance, the consultant was invited again a few years later. Sometimes there were long-standing relationships, which endured over time.

Some Persistent Difficulties

It was always difficult to meet all members of staff together. A consultant desires this at least two or three times in the course of a project.

There were difficulties in being accepted by all stakeholders. The consultant may have been chosen for a variety of reasons–which had their own repercussions with different stakeholders. If the CEO wanted a consultant, the board was reluctant and vice versa. Much of the floating distrust had to be dealt with as the process unfolded. Sometimes the strength of top management support at the entry stage could itself become a liability when building trust within the layers in the organisation.

The consultants usually seemed to work in pairs–often a man and a woman. There was also a perceived or accepted hierarchy between the two consultants in their own minds and in the client's mind. Very often the consultants experienced splitting processes where one of them became 'good' and the other 'bad'. Such processes led to the consultants' giving up their roles and moving to other modes of functioning. Sometimes the personal agendas of the consultants came in, to shift them into other modes of operation.

There were also perceptions as well as the real danger of the consultant being used as a tool for some particular constituency. Entry at the behest of the donor made their intent suspect. As the process unfolded, one or the other segment in the organisation tried to make the consultants the holders of their agenda. For example, the board, the CEO or the staff union.

It was also a major challenge to keep up the schedule of activities and maintain the initial enthusiasm when frequent changes were made and there was often a process drift.

Defining the steps in the task contract with provision for being flexible and making the effort to hold on to the schedule is a challenge.

Views of Client Systems

Key persons from four major organisations shared their perspectives about bringing in an OD consultant.

They would like OD to be part of their organisational life, because it resonates with the humanistic values, which they espouse. Sometimes they are concerned whether the consultant truly understands their passion and their particular political stance towards their work. The cost of consultancy is also a factor. They hold their organisations very close to their hearts and find it tough to expose their internal dynamics to an outsider's gaze. The challenging tasks taken up leave little time for pausing or reflecting on the internal dynamics. They have found various ways to accept OD inputs despite these anxieties.

- To take sporadic advice and work on it in their own way.
- To call in different consultants to look at different aspects and then integrate the findings to plan change.
- To have a long-term relationship with a consultant, redefining the task of the consultancy as the context shifted.
- To take sporadic inputs, and try to build HR and people management systems to suit their values and vision.

They were all of the view that sound HR practices have to be built in before engaging in an OD exercise. These views gave the practitioners some food for thought.

Academic Viewpoint

OD practitioners could see an intervention as one of the events in the evolution of an organisation. This would give them a more phenomenological understanding of the organisation and its place within a larger social system. The OD frameworks discussed were positivist in their flavour. They seemed to work on the assumption that changes within the organisation was an adequate response to the imbalances they perceived. There was a danger in overlooking the contextual trends. These projects were happening in a context where non-governmental organisations (NGOs) themselves were no longer anti-establishment in a manner fashionable before the globalisation era. Developing case studies for building professionalism in the practice of OD could be a way forward at this stage.

Post Conference Work

There was considerable enthusiasm for participating in the development of case studies with offers from nine consultants to share their work. This led to the next phase of work towards developing case studies to meet the learning need of professionals in this sector. It was envisaged that the writing of case studies would be completed by September 2006. The writing however took longer than anticipated and the drafts were ready by February 2007.

Overview of the Case Studies

It was agreed that these case studies were being written to share experiences with newcomers to OD work aspiring to build their facilitation and intervention skills. The framework for documentation can be seen in Appendix 1.1.

The case studies are composed of three elements, namely a narrative report on the activities, a reflective essay by the consultants on the challenges faced during the change process, and a review of the aspects that have been retained and absorbed in the organisation by another OD practitioner. We have tried to bring in a degree of uniformity across the case studies and still retain the individual style and flavour. It was fortunate that Rolf and Ronken Lynton consented to work on the case studies. They facilitated the dialogue among the case writers and reviewers. Each case was read and discussed threadbare.

Case Study Summary

A brief outline of each study is presented here.

Case I—Bringing in Social Perspectives to a Technically Oriented Programme

The study relates to the four-year-long effort to inculcate more participative styles of working among staff members and community participation in programme choices. The efforts of the consultant met with initial success but were resisted when the diagnosis did not match the mental models about the organisation cherished by the top management. The challenge faced by the consultant in dealing with complexity in a large system that expresses its resistance is highlighted in this study.

Case II—Experimentation with Collective Leadership in a Small Organisation

The author vividly captures the anxieties in a high-profile NGO when the founder leader decides to leave and the next tier of leadership within the organisation struggles to evolve a collective leadership model. The study brings out the support needed from the governance structure to foster changes of this nature. The consultant then has to recognise the gaps between the espoused and the practised norms and work to reduce them.

Case III—Re-working Identity to Facilitate Change

This case study discusses the challenges in reworking the gendered perspectives of roles both within and outside the organisation to enhance impact. The consultants describe their efforts and the relative ease with which the organisation was able to change its ways of working with women's groups in their project. They also describe the stronger resistance to actually address the gender-based role definition and the challenge of recruiting and retaining women on their staff. The challenge of nudging organisations to look within even while they change others stands out clearly in this piece.

Case IV—Democratisation of Access to Common Resources through Process-based Reform

This study shares the challenges of working with the technical cadres in a bureaucracy bringing in the perspectives of the various stakeholders with special emphasis on issues of marginalisation and vulnerability. It demonstrates the possibilities of working with bureaucratic systems by foregrounding the political dimensions of liberalisation and administrative reforms, and trusting the humanness of all stakeholders. The very language of OD seems problematic for the facilitators who see themselves as partners rather than consultants.

Case V—Revival of a Chronic Loss-making Rural Financial Institution

This presents a 'classic' intervention in a relatively large system with focus on financial viability through the strengthening of social perspectives embedded in the organisation's design. The consultants had to work with a group of change agents to build collaboration and cohesion around the organisation's core task. Working through the assumptions and mental models of the staff members and pushing in diagnosis and strategy to the branch level were the key challenges. One special aspect here was doing the balancing act between the expert and the facilitator role in a manner that builds self-reliance within the system.

APPENDIX 1.1: THE FRAMEWORK FOR C-POD DOCUMENTATION

The frameworks developed and used for documentation in this project have been elaborated here.

Documenting Consultant-client Relationship by Contributors

You are invited to share your experiences of working on a project, which went through the various stages of an OD process listed here:

- Entry,
- Developing the contract,
- Data collection and diagnosis,
- Presenting the diagnosis,
- Design of interventions,
- Initiating action and
- Assessing the impact.

Your feelings, thoughts and actions as the process moved through these stages and your reflections on how this impacted the flow of work; the client's feelings as you saw them and your efforts to engage with these feelings; the dynamics within the OD team in its interactions with the client system; as well as your experiences with various stakeholders would all be relevant and of interest.

While a brief description of the client organisation will be necessary to set the context for the reader, elaborate information on the client system will not be necessary. On the whole this could be a write-up of about 10-12 A4 size pages, font size 12.

This write-up should be accompanied by a documentation of the methodologies used, with some details as to what went right and what needs further refinement.

Mid-course Process Review for Reviewers

OD team members can use this form for change management teams to track key processes while they are engaged in an intervention. (This is a comprehensive list and all organisations may not simultaneously plan change in all these areas.) Each member of the team should first fill it individually. Some key executive role holders may also be asked to fill the form as a reality check.

The responses should then be compared. Any variations in perceptions should be discussed within the team–such variations could provide important clues for mid-course corrections. Changes and corrections can be planned on the basis of these reviews. The individual reports can be consolidated into a periodic process review. It could be taken up every six months.

Review of the Scheduled Activities

Describe the major activities that took place in the following areas.

1. Improving clarity about purpose, goals, plans for activities.
2. Strengthening managerial processes of planning and organising day-to-day tasks, resource identification and deployment.

3. HR processes like recruitment, induction, career planning for individuals, performance appraisal and feedback and compensation benefits.
4. Organisation-wide changes in structure, communication processes, delegation of power and authority, role clarification and leadership development.
5. Improving relationships with key stakeholders–community, funders, donors.
6. Absorbing technological innovations, for example, IT support or changed ways of managing key tasks.
7. Any other tasks planned.

If you were to re-do any of these activities, how would you do them differently? Classify the initiatives in terms of what you see as their effectiveness.

1. Interventions which went very well (that is, according to the change management teams' expectations and had the desired impact).
2. Interventions which have been completed, but you don't yet feel the impact.
3. Interventions which have not had the desired impact.

What were the factors that were supporting the change process?
What were the factors that were hindering the change process?
Any surprising outcomes or unanticipated changes?
Personally speaking, what did you enjoy the most in all these activities?
What did you find the most difficult or challenging?
Name, date and location.

A Framework for Reviewing OD Programmes

This framework, to outline core processes in a change management programme, is recommended as a summary that captures the essence. Some aspects may not be relevant for all organisations.

It should therefore be used in an appropriate manner and should be accompanied by detailed reporting as well.

Only the relevant aspects could be commented upon.

1. What triggered the OD process–any specific event or a regular pattern?
2. How did the OD process get people across the organisation to revisit the organisation's core purpose?
3. What were the changes identified in the following key processes?

- Organisation-wide integrating processes.
- Revisiting and refining of goals, vision or core purpose.
- Recognising core areas of interest and competence.
- Articulating ways in which members of the organisation will work with each other and their client systems (process values or culture).
- Internal communication.
- Roles, teamwork, interactions and coordination among teams across locations/functions.
- Service delivery.

  (*i*) Redefining clients and users and their needs.
  (*ii*) Re-designing the service delivery systems to improve impact and effectiveness.

- Managerial aspects.

  (*i*) Resource support needed and available.
  (*ii*) Planning of activities and programmes.
  (*iii*) Setting goals for teams and individuals.
  (*iv*) Recruitment, induction, compensation benefits, reward and punishment.
  (*v*) Staff development.
  (*vi*) Information management (with IT support).

- Processes to engage the individual.

  (*i*) Leadership processes.
  (*ii*) Mutual support.

(*iii*) Opportunities for growth and development (professional, positional, etc.).

4. What were the changes introduced in structure, systems and processes?
5. How was it ensured that they go together and with the overall spirit of the change programme?
6. How were the decisions about the changes arrived at? (Formal and informal contributions of external consultant, client groups and other stakeholders, top management, middle mangers, front line staff, etc., in the decision-making).
7. How were the ideas of these changes generated, developed, communicated to staff and clients and embedded within the organisation?
8. How do these changes work together? Any inconsistencies that have to be managed?
    - And dilemmas/apparent contradictions which have to be held together? (The creative tension in the organisation?)
    - What were the older ways which have been given up?
    - Any procedures which have been simplified or improved upon?
9. Resistance that came up, to what extent was it handled and how?
   Was it expected, unexpected/any major surprises?
10. Who are the internal advocates of change? Top management, a few change agents, team leaders, or resource persons?
11. How does the change programme address the social concerns that the organisation carries–what impact will it have in the context of the environment, for example, how will it affect others doing similar work or the relationship of the organisation with the community.

2

C-POD II

SHAIBAL GUHAROY

Nine people, five cases, two amazing days of interaction and learning–that was C-POD II, organised during 13 and 14 February 2007.

Sponsored by the Sir Ratan Tata Trust, the nine organisational development (OD) practitioners, all with years of actual field experience, had gathered at the idyllic Satyam Technology Centre facility near Hyderabad, to exchange and share their experiences, thoughts and ideas.

The participants were, in alphabetical order, Ashok Singha, Ganesh Anantharaman, Haritha Sharma, K.S.S. Rau, Lalitha Iyer, Pradip Prabhu, Pratap J. Das, Shirish Joshi and V. Suresh. Eminent Professors Rolf and Ronken Lynton in their extensive travels, had graciously accepted the invitation and made themselves available during the period, to act as guides and facilitators for the workshop.

Conducted in the appropriately named '*Dronacharya*' conference hall, the workshop got off to a warm start, as people walked in, greeting friends and colleagues, and above all, happy to see the two professors.

The formal introductions over, the team went straight ahead with the job at hand–to discuss the five case studies that they had worked on and were willing now to submit to peer review, get feedback, share ideas, thoughts, the joys, pains, successes and failures.

On the first day, three case studies were taken up and the participants were split into teams of three members each. Each group got to study a case and its review over the next hour or so and analyse and discuss it amongst themselves. On consensus, the participants agreed to move out of the room, to the lush lawns outside, around the very inviting swimming pool, to sit on the grass, or under the trees, to carry on with the work at hand.

The groups went through the assigned case studies and took turns reading them aloud, before making notes of the various points of doubts and questions, that they felt needed more explanation/expansion. Once that part was over and after an exquisite lunch the team met again in the conference room.

The case studies were now taken up, one by one, and the questions asked, clarifications sought, both of the OD facilitator and the reviewer–about the organisation, the problem that led to the entry of the facilitator and the work done, questions about his brief, how he initiated the process and went about it, clarifications about the methods and his analysis of the organisation and the results of his work. The reviewer was also asked for clarifications on the points of his observations, the depth (or lack of it) of impact of the whole OD process, and so on.

The second day was taken up by discussions on the remaining two cases. It followed the same pattern, except that this time all participants went through the cases and then discussed the various aspects of the cases, their results and the reviewers' reports.

The candid discussions led to the revelation of a common set of emotions that each OD practitioner invariably experienced–that of the initial 'encounter' with the 'monolith' of the organisation; the 'breaking' of ideals and expectations; the importance of understanding and respecting the intricate warps and wefts of personal and people relationship within that 'monolith'; the Facilitator's anxieties and doubts about the challenges, the hard work, the trials and tribulations; and the final joy or disappointment at the end of the process.

His feelings of helplessness or happiness depended on the response to, or outcome of, his suggestions and efforts, or the frustration that followed the administration's irrational resistance to accept change. The tremendous level of satisfaction arose when the organisation agreed to adapt, or at least acknowledged, the need to adjust, or, just changed their perception of the problem that had brought the Facilitator to their organisation.

The discussions uncovered the realisation that these monolithic and patriarchal institutions had a deep understanding and desire to change with time. And yet, a few were either unable, or unwilling, for various reasons, to effect this change, becoming extremely sensitive to even a hint of criticism. Fiercely paternal, some were aggressively defensive, even resenting the whole OD intervention process, which they themselves had invited.

Other aspects that came to the fore were the facilitators' understanding of the social impact of their work, and therefore the responsibility they shouldered; and their understanding and appreciation of the differences between 'gender mainstreaming' and 'gender sensitising', and the meaning and difficulties of implementing it in the field.

It was realised that it was humans, (individuals with emotions and egos), that they were dealing with, and not an inanimate 'entity', and therefore there could be no 'set rule', nor a 'standardisation' of methods and tools. Each case and each situation required innovation and adaptation, while remaining sensitive to the various levels and individuals involved. And it was most important to remain alert so as not to become, unwittingly, a mere pawn in the larger power game of the organisation!

On a lighter note, there was also a lively debate about the usage and ethics of using modern technology and gadgets for orientation purpose in OD interventions.

Another important outcome was the retrospection on the cases by the facilitator, a 're-thought' about how it may have been different, whether he should have enquired further, deeper, and thus avoided some of the pitfalls of the internal power-structure and politics of the organisation.

With their learned and sage advice, thoughtful inputs, suggestions, encouragement and support, and the nuggets of personal experience, the presence of Professors Rolf and Ronken Lynton was comforting and calming.

3

Case I—Ekta

Swimming with the Tide*

A Case Study Prepared under the C-POD Project for SRTT

The Context and the Institutions Involved

(Compiled by the C-POD Team)

Ekta Development Research Foundation (or Ekta) is a well-known organisation working in rural development for over 35 years. The founder started the work in a village in a major southern state, and it slowly spread to over ten states of India through sister organisations.

The organisation is renowned for introducing technology in rural livelihoods with the 'doorstep delivery' approach and is now also working in areas such as agriculture-horticulture, watershed, health and women empowerment. Ekta has a strong human resource base with high techno-managerial capabilities, employing over 2000 people. Based on its various experiences, it is now propagating a cluster development approach to enhance the livelihood of identified poor families with the help of a variety of appropriate livelihood interventions, reaching out to over two million rural families.

---

* The intervention process was conducted during April 2002 to March 2006. The review was conducted in December 2006.

The role of Ekta evolved over a period of time, and they adapted themselves to the changing environment. A major bilaterally funded project for the transfer of technologies for sustainable development supported Ekta to undertake a formal organisational development (OD) process. The efforts were initiated with the help of a British consultant. The process did not take shape because a clear theme for the change effort was not readily identifiable. Later on it was felt that involving an Indian consultant would be more appropriate.

Some of the issues that were of concern to Ekta at that time were:

- The senior technical staff were feeling neglected.
- There was no clearly defined career-plan, thus progressive and competent staff members were uncertain about their future prospects in the organisation.
- In the absence of a formal HRD manual, many felt that there was no transparency in the decision-making process.
- In the absence of a clear work-plan and measurement of output, they felt that their performance was not being assessed properly.
- Ekta had a very small HRD division, conversant with personnel administration rather than HRD.

They invited Manoj, an independent OD consultant with a rich corporate experience and a great interest in development praxis, as facilitator. The effort was initiated in April 2002 and continued till March 2006. As facilitator for the overall change process, Manoj designed and facilitated a variety of interventions over the four-year period and gradually became so involved that, as the processes neared completion, there was an invitation, and even an expectation, of his becoming a full-time executive with Ekta. But that did not happen.

In December 2006, a reviewer visited Ekta for two days to gain an understanding of the ways in which the organisation had been able to integrate the learning from the OD process. Though it was acknowledged that the various interventions had been effective and had impacted the organisation positively, the reluctance of the leadership to revisit the experiences and the level of anger towards the facilitator came as a surprise.

The following narrative offers some clues to tapping the change sutras for generating the energy and will for change and demonstrates the after-effects of articulating that sutra for the client. It offers insights into when, and how much of, the diagnosis should be offered to client systems and in what language. At another level it brings out the struggles of self-image of the exceptionally brilliant individuals who have sacrificed their personal careers for the cause of development, and the reality of NGOs that had to compromise on their effectiveness for the sake of financial viability. It also highlights the 'illegitimacy' associated with financial viability of NGOs, as they are expected to be primarily altruistic. The change facilitator is constantly living with the knowledge that when we do what we do, we may have consequences we did not anticipate.

The OD Event Structure

(*Based on Formal Documentation*)

The Organisational Structure of Ekta

Ekta is in reality a group of organisations with the parent organisation being the Development Research Foundation. The relationship between the head office and the state societies is as follows:

- While one Ekta trustee is the chairman of the society, a vice president (VP) is the executive vice chairman (EVC).
- Ekta employees are deputed to societies for taking up senior management positions like PD (programme directors)/chief programme coordinators/project managers, and so on.

Figure 3.1 The Organisational Structure of Ekta

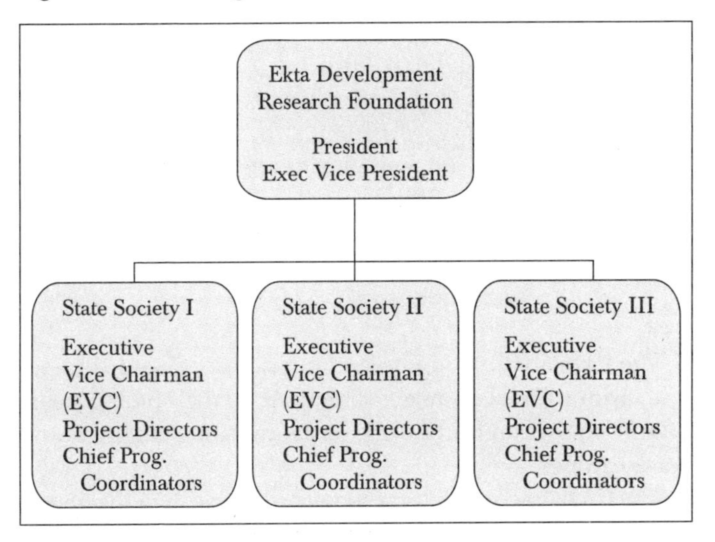

Manoj was supported in his efforts by an internal team of two women, Ms Shuba and Ms Neeta, and the process was kicked off through a meeting called EKTA 2010.

EKTA 2010

This was the initial diagnostic exploration initiated so that a sustainable OD effort could emerge out of the envisioning of a preferred future and exploration of choices by a participatory process, involving significant role holders. This forum was envisaged as a gathering of all members of the core management groups (CMGs) of vice presidents of Ekta and a cross section of executives across various locations, projects, sister organisations, levels of hierarchy and age groups. The meeting was conducted at the Ekta Training Facility in July 2002. Twenty-three members from the organisation participated and four members, including the consultant, anchored the process. The meeting was designed on the large scale interactive process (LSIP) model.

The objectives of the meeting were:

- To understand the emerging trends in the development sector.
- To envision a preferred future for Ekta.
- To make choices about actions today, to see results over the next three years.

The participants were invited to brainstorm and come to conclusions about strategic directions in the coming years within the overall framework of the mission statement and shared values.

The CMG members were requested to use their discretion and select a few issues for further action and they short-listed seven issues. The decision was based on the ratings received, as well as the concerns of the CMG members. New groups were formed to work on the action plan for these priority issues. The members were given the choice of selecting a group as per their interest. It was ensured that each group had representation of CMG members, field staff and staff from head office. Majority of the participants felt that the meeting was successful in identifying the relevant issues and discussing the various aspects involved. At the end of the meeting it was decided that the CMG would take the lead to declare a timetable for action on the final seven points discussed.

CMG Meeting on OD Process

The first CMG meeting after EKTA 2010 was held in August. The main conclusions of the meeting were:

- Ekta needs to improve the sustainability and financial viability of its core programmes.
- Ekta should be in a position to spot new opportunities and constantly work for experimenting in new areas, new technologies, and new interventions.
- Ekta needs to focus on organisational development, particularly with respect to succession planning and induction of professional talent.

It was decided that three initiatives, namely revised performance appraisal system, 360-degree feedback, and assessment/development centres would be launched before March 2003 for all existing EC members. The assessment centres would also be extended to an identified group of 25–30 people who were seen as potential successors to the key positions. The group also looked at success experiences as well as failed efforts of Ekta in its core programmes. The key success factors of Ekta were identified as:

- Centralised design and decentralised implementation,
- Strong research base, and
- Technical and managerial manpower at the headquarter and extension-oriented manpower at the field level.

It was decided that the OD effort would focus on enhancing these strengths.

Intervention Cycle

Figure 3.2 The Intervention Cycle for Ekta

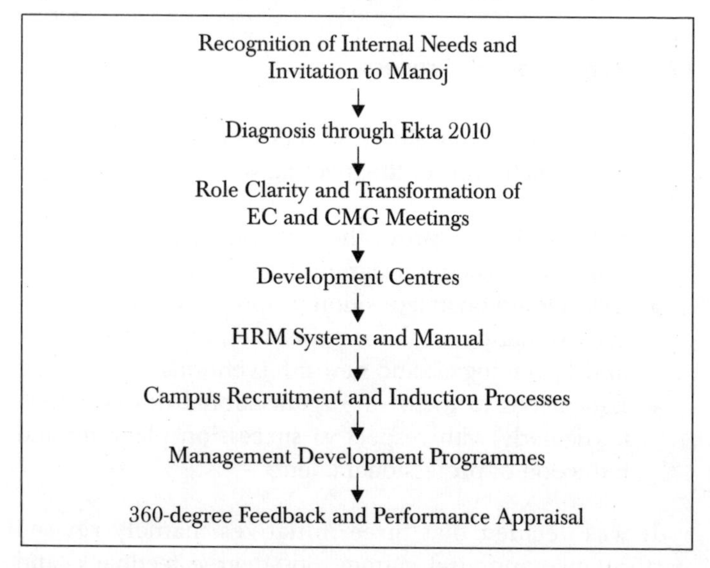

A variety of interventions carried out over the next few years were:

Clarification on the Roles/Functions of EC and CMG

Manoj facilitated practically all the meetings of CMG (around twenty meetings of two-day duration), and EC (around ten meetings of four-day duration) between 2002 and 2006. A wide variety of issues were raised, discussed and decided upon at these meetings. Manoj's role was to initiate discussions by maximising participation of members, raise issues and offer his views and suggestions. The CMG, and the president, with his accommodative and pragmatic approach, were able to arrive at an appropriate resolution on the issues. Manoj did not enjoy any formal authority in the organisation, all decisions being taken by the appropriate organisational authorities such as the CMG, the EC, the president, etc. Some of the key decisions are listed here.

- EC was converted into a forum for learning and information sharing, consultation and a think tank. The CMG was formally legitimised as the apex decision-making body. The trustees approved the changes in the role of the EC and CMG.
- The decentralisation manual was amended. Through this change the administrative heads of societies were empowered to take most day-to-day decisions in the areas of purchase, financial management and legal compliances for the society. The role of EVC was restricted to the approval of quarterly budgets for expenditure, acquisition of capital and human resources. This gave VPs the necessary time to perform their new corporate roles. Another round of decentralisation of authority in the society after two years was approved.
- The design of one of the key programmes was modified through the formation of theme-wise subgroups. The other subgroups gathered the best practices of another programme and developed a manual. Decisions were also taken to strengthen the Community-Based Organisations.
- Some sensitive HR issues like enhancement of pension benefits and selective increase in retirement age were discussed and decided upon.
- Issues like approach to investment in assets were thoroughly debated.
- Drafts of three-year plans of sister organisations, along with the changing profile of staffing patterns, renegotiations of the relationship between Ekta and sister organisations, were discussed and decided upon.
- Strategy for Ekta's expansion into new states and union territories were discussed and certain decisions

regarding transfer of staff and formation of new legal entities were taken.

- Ekta's relationship with the community organisations floated by it was discussed and efforts made in different sister organisations to evolve a mutually beneficial relationship, wherein the Community Based Organisations (CBOs) would be able to afford a small group of Ekta employees on their payrolls.

In addition, the EC engaged in self-reflective processes like using the International Development Research Centre (IDRC), Canada organisational effectiveness framework and relating it to Ekta. Different societies, in addition to presenting their achievements, also described some of their failures. Some of the identified officers, as well as a few promising women officers (though junior), were invited to various EC meetings to help them get a first-hand feel of the organisational issues and processes.

HR Policy Manual

Circulars regarding HR policies were issued from time to time. The need to review many of these policies was felt in order to attract and retain talent. A comprehensive HRD manual was prepared in consultation with the EC members, as well as HR and finance heads of the state societies. This manual was formally approved by the CMG, and some of the key features of the new policies were:

Flexibility in Employment

To attract specialists, project/contract appointment terms were made more attractive as compared to permanent employees. Part-time employment option was also created. A policy was formalised for post-retirement working.

Remuneration

In its initial years, the remuneration structure at Ekta was close to government pay scales, but over a period of time, particularly from 1985 onwards (after the Fourth Pay Commission), Ekta's salaries did not increase in line with those of the government. On the other hand, due to non-differentiated salary revision policies, salaries of some of the support staff were quite competitive, while those of qualified professionals were way below the market levels.

To partially correct this situation certain measures were adopted over a period of time. Performance-based differentiation was introduced through a scheme of annual one-time payment. Allowances meant for attracting professional staff were substantially enhanced and linked to their performance over the previous three years. A few staff members, at various levels, were picked up for salary rationalisation through a participatory process. Entry-level salaries for qualified professionals were enhanced so that reasonable remuneration could be offered during campus recruitment. Proportionate adjustment for existing employees was done on a case-to-case basis. Confirmed employees were allowed 15 days of outside work like consultancy in a year to augment their remuneration. The scheme for reimbursement of hospitalisation expenses was upgraded to provide enhanced cover, particularly for critical diseases.
A policy on dealing with sexual harassment issues was added.

Development Centres (DCs)

Development Centres (DCs)* were conducted for a 45-member group drawn from Ekta staff and its associate societies as part of OD efforts with the help of the Behaviour Science

---

* Development Centre is a methodology or approach to assess competencies of individual participants based on psychometric research.

Centre in Mumbai. The main objective of conducting the DC was to identify members who were capable of taking up higher responsibilities in the organisation.

The DCs helped in defining and mapping the competencies of the top three layers in Ekta. They offered feedback to the participants and helped them to plan their own development. They also provided inputs for designing management development programmes (MDPs). The results prepared by the DCs were used as inputs for promoting and placing individuals, so that they could perform roles that were aligned to their potential.

360-degree Feedback

The need for an open feedback system within the teams was increasingly felt. The methodology of 360-degree feedback seemed to go well with the philosophy of Ekta. It was decided that the CMG members would undergo the process first, and then the EC members. TVRLS, based in Ahmedabad, designed the questionnaire. The participants received feedback from superiors, peers, and subordinates. The choice of getting feedback from external partners, such as government officers and donor agencies was given to participants. This process was the first formal effort to get a feedback from subordinates and peers. Later on many subordinates reported favourable changes in the behaviour of their seniors.

Campus Recruitment and Induction

After a gap of almost 15 years, Ekta attempted centralised campus recruitment in 2003. These recruits were from agriculture, horticulture and animal husbandry departments from reputed universities. But due to a variety of reasons, Ekta could not retain most of them. Learning from this experience, a batch of 10 students was recruited from rural management and social work backgrounds from campuses. Encouraged by the revised process more recruitments were planned for the future. Some lessons learnt in the process have been listed here.

- The initial classroom training should be very short (two-three weeks), and more participatory. Methods like 'synergogy' (Mouton and Blake, 1984) yielded very good results.
- The induction in the field should be gradual, through projects that involve intense field interaction and support from experts. This helps in bridging the gap between the academic world and field realities.
- The trainees should be posted at district level towns or society headquarters and the assignments given to build on their educational background.

Management Development Programmes (MDPs)

Based on the DCs feedback, along with further deliberations, management development inputs were planned. Thirty-six members attended and enthusiastically participated in the programmes. On the one hand, it assured Ekta a pipeline of field managers (generalists); it also gave confidence to the CMG to manage the succession requirements by promoting its under-utilised middle managers rather than looking for external recruits.

Similar programmes were planned for existing finance professionals (for economic analysis) and specialists (for research and consultancy).

Composite Impact of the Interventions

The impact of various OD initiatives can be summarised as follows:

- Ekta had already been practising participatory approach in rural development over the past few years; the OD effort now enhanced that participatory process inside the organisation itself by encouraging EC members to generate a variety of suggestions and views on institutional and programmatic issues. These then became the inputs for the final decisions to be taken by the CMG.
- Ekta succeeded in acknowledging its organisational culture, as it was, without being overly critical or defensive about it. This helped the management to work towards fully replicating its efforts through its three core programmes and cluster development approach. Ekta became more confident in acting as a multi-state, large-scale implementation organisation, with strong research support and input production facilities. It also graduated towards utilising other models of engagement, like acting as a resource agency or only as an input supplier.
- While emphasising its financial viability, Ekta revamped one of its core programmes to make it more relevant to the community needs and be more self-reliant by fixing a service charge.
- Ekta started to revive its emphasis on the economic well-being of its employees. It also actively engaged in the efforts of attracting younger talent and developing and empowering its existing field managers.

Further Agenda

Ekta needs to take many of the change initiatives to their logical conclusions by implementing them in all field locations appropriately. Participatory and facilitative process needed to be strengthened much more. Like many other NGOs, Ekta had not been able to retain qualified and articulate professionals beyond a few years. Though Ekta tried to integrate gender issues in many of its field level programmes, it is still unable to attract and retain women employees in any significant proportion.

Each of the societies has learnt to survive as an independent organisation. The senior team needs to consolidate this operational freedom by complementing and building on the strengths of one another. They need to learn to creatively challenge and support each other simultaneously.

Reflections of the Facilitator

Keen on doing some work in the development sector, I had met Dr Ram, the president of Ekta. But our meeting proved inconclusive until I received a call from Mr Tandon, the executive vice president (EVP). He wanted to explore the possibility of hiring me as a consultant for OD in Ekta.

Soon a meeting between Dr Ram, Mr Tandon and I followed, where the following points were discussed.

- The first step for a serious OD effort should be to develop a preferred organisational vision, say for 2010.
- This vision can then be developed through a participatory process involving a cross section of employees, as well as various stakeholders. This would surface issues pertaining to the difference between preferred future vis-à-vis current realities, and the possible ways of reaching the preferred future. The suggestions could cover changes in HR policies, as well as many other areas.
- A strong, top management support would be necessary for the success of this endeavour.
- Two senior management staff and I would periodically review the progress of the OD effort.

To my joy and pleasant surprise, they both readily agreed to my suggestions, and it was decided that about 30 employees of the various groups of the organisation would be called for a six-day meeting. To prepare for the meeting, I decided to understand Ekta in the following ways:

- Reading literature–I read two small books, on the founder and the history of Ekta. I also read a report on the evolution of Ekta as an institution.
- Interviews–I met and interviewed some senior functionaries at their head office and interacted with 20–25 functionaries at various levels.
- Interactions–I visited two research stations, two sister organisation head offices, three field offices, accompanying field workers and meeting participating communities in small groups, and individually.

I attended the executive committee (EC) meeting, the apex decision-making forum of Ekta, consisting of the President, vice presidents, heads of state societies and heads of programmes. I also read the minutes of the EC meetings for the preceding two years, as well as reports of some of the taskforces related to HR/OD issues of the organisation.

My preparation through these secondary data, interviews and observations provided me with insights into the many articulated, as well as unarticulated strengths and weaknesses of Ekta and its programmes, and I could understand the institutional issues within. I also got a first-hand feel of the different schools of thought, and the inter-generational differences that existed within the organisation. I could understand the dynamics of the different groupings around subjects and approaches; and the tension points between these groups. It also helped me appreciate the scope and variety of the organisation's programmes and projects, initiated or funded by major international donors. Thus, I got to know the organisation better, different parts of the structure slowly came to the fore, and I started visualising it in its entirety.

Though I did not make a formal presentation on my 'diagnosis', I was able to utilise my insights for the EKTA 2010 vision-building workshop to articulate many issues, which led to further debate.

During the preparation, I realised that the OD effort, to be successful, couldn't be steered solely by Dr Ram or Mr Tandon, but needed the active participation of all the vice presidents who ran the various state societies. Ekta had gone through a major financial crisis in the mid-1980s following which each of the vice presidents had practically managed their societies independently. Though there was still a lot of centralisation of authority, there was a decentralisation of power, thus making it a multi-polar organisation. Any substantive change would thus require wide-ranging deliberations and building of broad consensus. Unlike the corporate sector, there were no competitive pressures here, and the leader of the organisation, Dr Ram, with his friendly and non-imposing style of functioning, was first among equals, vis-à-vis his other colleagues.

The Change *Sutra*

My training and experience in OD had led me to believe that every organisation has a governing *sutra* (key principle). If the change initiative is built on this *sutra*, it can be easily implemented. I had studied the history of organisational changes in Ekta to be in touch with this *sutra*, and had deliberations in the CMG on identifying initiatives that had succeeded and those that had failed. Some of the lessons learnt by these exercises are:

- Ekta being a highly centralised organisation, a lot of deliberation went on among experts at the central level, while a lot of experimentation happened at the field level before a programme or approach took shape, and they were sure that a 'perfect' model had been built. Only then did the programme get implemented through their dedicated field staff. Thus, the broad pattern is centralised decision-making and decentralised implementation.
- They placed a lot of value on rigorous experimentation and generating valid information by using the methods of physical sciences. They were not very adept, or comfortable, with methods of social and behavioural sciences.

Box 3.1 A Scientific Orientation

> The Development Centre exercise was seen as inherently risky, because it might damage the morale of the middle management. The idea was accepted once it was demonstrated through statistical analysis that these assessment results were not biased against those who were not fluent in English, had longer field experience, or were coming from non-management backgrounds.

- Being a hierarchical organisation, once the subordinates got a hint of what the boss thought, they avoided all discussions or suggestions. On the other hand, if the boss made a decision, or an organisational circular was issued, the implementation was very smooth.
- Senior officers, being very dedicated to the organisation, had made personal sacrifices to ensure continuity and financial viability. This concern for continued sustainability and corpus building also had its downside, with officers, at times, over-focusing on the financial viability of the organisation. This brought in an undue conservatism; in fact, 'financial viability' was the underlying sutra of most key decisions.

This concern was making the organisation inward looking, focussed on its own viability and assets; accepting sub-optimal programmes primarily for their saving potential. On the other hand, if Ekta concerned itself with the financial viability of all its stakeholders, that is, the community, field workers, CBOs, and so on, it could in fact create and sustain a 'win-win' situation. It could also minimise or eliminate initial subsidies/grants by making the programmes commercially viable propositions for all concerned.

Redefining Mental Models

Many of these characteristics of Ekta did not conform to my idea of a 'voluntary organisation'. I believed that a voluntary organisation should be non-hierarchical, decentralised, flexible, participatory and unconcerned about its own viability. I had to struggle with myself in understanding and appreciating Ekta as it was, rather than, as it should be. Though the situation has changed now, the fact that Ekta had gone through a major financial crisis about 20 years earlier had left a scar in the collective memory of the system. The emphasis on financial viability was possibly a result of that experience. This realisation prompted a re-think on my approach. So while proposing the change agenda as its philosophical/logical justification, I emphasised on the impact it would have on their financial viability. This made the selling of 'change' very easy.

As I started to look at the characteristics, as given, I started finding ways of getting around the dysfunctionalities, thereby avoiding unintended negative consequences. I had to struggle a lot with myself so as not to work on reducing weaknesses but instead enhance and multiply what was healthy and functional. Though I did not use 'appreciative inquiry' technique, I made conscious efforts to have an appreciative orientation.

Finding Freedom within Constraints

There were several occasions when I had to find ways to move ahead despite the barriers. Let me illustrate.

I was told that the EC is the apex decision-making body of the organisation. Yet my discussions with the members revealed that issues raised by the EC usually remained pending. Taskforces got appointed but nothing much happened thereafter. On the other hand the top management imposed many decisions on the EC. The decision-making process was not perceived to be transparent enough. My observations of the EC meeting made me feel that the EC was more of a ratification body than a decision-making body. Most members remained silent during discussions, even where inputs were required.

I learnt that there was one more forum called CMG consisting of six to seven vice presidents which was the real decision-making body. Issues got informally discussed in the CMG, and after arriving at a consensus these decisions were put up to the EC for ratification. A study of the history of the EC structure revealed that it had consisted of only six to seven members during the days of the founder. However after his death the president felt the need of broad-basing the consultative process. This led to the growth of the EC to about 18 to 20 members. While it enhanced sharing and learning across states, and included inputs from programme specialists, it also made the decision-making process more complex, leading to the creation of the smaller and informal group called 'CMG'.

Clarity and Structure

With this knowledge, and the consent of the trustees to formally transform the CMG into an apex decision-making forum, the EC was retained as an experience and knowledge management platform. Issues would now first get discussed in the EC, without committing to any resolution; the CMG members would then take cognisance of the various views expressed before arriving at a final decision. Since the CMG members were accountable for the performance of their respective organisations, they would decide on the issues; so the decision-making authority got aligned with accountability.

Influencing the Culture

The new arrangement, though clean and elegant on paper, was still not working, as very few people spoke at the full EC meetings. So we changed the method of discussion; the EC was broken into smaller groups, which were then expected to debate/discuss issues before putting up their opinions as a group in front of the EC. This seemed to work partially, as it was easier to share a 'group's' views, instead of an individual view.

But still, something was lacking. Further observations revealed that even in the small groups, where CMG members were present, people were not opening up. To overcome this, the CMG members worked as a separate sub-group, while the other participants were divided into two or three groups. This led to a more intense discussion and generation of diverse viewpoints. The positive fallout of this exercise was that the quality of CMG discussions also improved as it got a preview of the various shades of opinion present in the senior management group. Thus the process became more transparent and participative at the same time ensuring accountability of the decision makers.

Multiple Roles

Within the HR/OD ambit I performed a variety of roles–a process facilitator, a counsellor, or an expert. I also took administrative responsibility of managing some of the initiatives like MDP, assessment centres, and so on and since it is a large and complex organisation, I had to personally relate to at least 20–25 people from different parts of the country. My involvement beyond OD was very helpful for this and travelling with people offered opportunities for closer interaction. These interactions helped me to appreciate and get influenced by the staff at various levels. Listening to their thoughts and emotions, consensus building, seeking of ideas, giving or receiving feedback became possible. Thus, apart from the formal roles, I was also playing the role of *Narad Muni.*

Insider–Outsider

At times I felt that I had the unique advantage of being both an insider and an outsider simultaneously. I was in touch with the pulse of the organisation because of my involvement beyond OD (I spent around eight to ten days per month for four years), yet on the other hand, when things were not moving fast enough I was not getting restless beyond a point as I had other preoccupations than Ekta.

Closure

The closure when it came was abrupt, taking me by surprise. I realised that there was a saturation of the OD effort, as whatever was possible, based on swimming with the tide, was being achieved. In fact the documentation of the OD experience aggravated the situation. My diagnosis of Ekta being a centralised and financial-viability oriented organisation was totally unacceptable to Mr Tandon. In my view, the documentation was technical in nature and the purpose of words like 'centralisation' was to describe the phenomenon, while the executive vice president (EVP) possibly saw this as an evaluation. In the current development jargon the whole description is politically incorrect and can be a serious hazard to the public image, and here I had failed in my judgement.

I had become very involved in the development work of Ekta instead of limiting myself to the OD process alone. I had recognised that in its form and style Ekta had a major role to play as an expert service provider to augment the efforts of the government particularly in remote areas for the benefit of tribal and small and medium farmers. Looking back over the four years I feel that much has changed and yet so much has remained the same. There was no mutation or transformation; there was a gradual and sustained evolution. Ekta has possibly become more aware of its own characteristics, and within broad parameters, was trying to realise its potential as a very large research and implementation organisation.

Postscript

(By the C-POD Team)

The closure itself and the reviewer's observations about the negativity expressed by the system, particularly about the contribution of the OD process and the facilitator, were very unsettling for Manoj. He was caught up with feelings of anger and sorrow simultaneously. He had very high respect for the EVP for his contribution, personal sacrifice and integrity. At the same time he was angry with him for belittling the contribution of the OD process, and by inference Manoj himself. To him it almost seemed to be a personal affront.

Manoj remains convinced that the basic diagnosis of financial viability, as the *sutra*, was valid. On reflection, he feels that he might have failed to demonstrate the positive possibilities associated with that *sutra* as mentioned above.

The EVP might have felt that his personal conviction and sacrifice was getting undermined if he was evaluated as working for an organisation that is focussed on its own financial viability. For Manoj the reality was that Ekta comprised a variety of people–some, like the EVP, have come in because they wanted to make a difference, while some others have come in because Ekta offered a job that was at par with a government job.

Internalising Change—An Assessment

(By the C-POD Reviewer–December 2006)

The purpose of my visit to Ekta was to review the OD process, with focus on what had taken root after the involvement had been discontinued. I also hoped to learn more about the OD process itself, while examining the ways in which some interventions have stuck and some have not.

Before starting, I studied the 'Reflections' paper by Manoj, which made fascinating reading. It made me curious to visualise the world of the facilitator and that of the client. I was looking forward to interacting with both. I spent two days at Ekta, discussing with the HR steering group in the headquarters and staff in the central research facility. I also had a discussion with Manoj about the processes and his perceptions of it. I offer my observations.

What Triggered the OD Process

The president and the executive vice president of Ekta wanted the services of Manoj, a well-known organisational development consultant, for doing OD work at Ekta. They had a series of meetings and the modalities were worked out.

Manoj received top management support for the OD work. It appears that before him other consultants had done some OD work at Ekta. However, this documentation was not shared with me.

How the OD Process got People across Ekta to Re-visit its Core Purpose

The OD process was fairly well spread over approximately four years. One intervention that was mentioned repeatedly both by the seniors and the juniors, was the Management Development Programmes (MDPs). These had the objectives of enhancing certain competencies, increasing knowledge and skills, discovering strengths in self and others and better relationship building. Indirectly, the learning made members hark back to the core purpose of the organisation.

Changes Identified in Some Key Processes

Manoj had facilitated several processes as listed here.

- EKTA 2010 meeting–focus was on shared understanding of key issues.
- Development centres–to identify members capable of taking on higher responsibilities in the organisation, and those who have potential to take up certain roles but need support for enhancing their abilities as a part of succession plan.
- A 360-degree feedback–wherein the members of the CMG underwent the process first followed by the members of the EC.
- MDPs–where the participants, through experiential learning, identified areas where they needed to build

their strengths anew for greater personal and organisational effectiveness.

Dr Ram shared his views on the various interventions in a separate communication. His views are summarised in Box 3.2.

Box 3.2 Views of Dr Ram

1. EKTA 2010 meeting: External experts from different fields were invited to share their experiences about Ekta. This was an important change which helped us to see beyond the limitations of the immediate situation and our own past.
2. Facilitation of EC meetings: Earlier, during the EC meetings, administrative matters and sharing of experiences, more in the form of reporting the programme, were discussed. Subsequently, we decided to utilise this as a forum for learning best practices and developing new themes.
3. Facilitation of CMG meetings: The facilitation helped us bring up various issues for discussion. Very often Manoj's views were considered as that of an outsider and impartial, and helped in taking correct decisions.
4. New HR policies: There were several matters which were practiced but not documented properly. Hence the decisions appeared *ad hoc.* With the focus on preparation of the HR manual, all the aspects were thoroughly reviewed and judicious decisions taken to formulate the HRD policy of the organisation.
5. Development centres: These not only helped in identifying the strengths and weaknesses, but also brought harmony and better understanding among the senior managers.
6. A 360-degree feedback: This type of feedback was never practiced earlier and proved to be very useful to the individual participants.
7. Induction programme for campus recruits: We took a bold decision of visiting campuses and offering our terms and conditions without hesitation.
8. MDP for senior managers: The course content was very well designed and appreciated. Also, very good resource persons were involved. The MDP really helped in strengthening our competency and in utilisation of internal staff for special jobs.

Residual Issues

I could sense some hostility towards my probing on the OD effort even in the first meeting with the HR steering group. This group has been constituted as a result of the discussions in the EC and further deliberations in the CMG. But there was no acknowledgement of Manoj's role in facilitating the deliberations that led to the creation of this structure. It was evident that Manoj's exit had not been on amicable terms.

A more detailed conversation with Mr Tandon, the EVP revealed that there was a lot more anger against the facilitator. He had difficulty in accepting Manoj's assessment of the impact of the interventions. He said that the 2010 Vision meeting did not have much significant impact. Similarly, he said that the DCs too were not much to go by. As for the 360-degree feedback, he said it was a novelty and people felt curious, but it did not last long. He said that the one intervention that had left a very positive impact was the MDP. He said that Ekta would conduct more MDPs, after modifying some inputs, so that there is a wider reach. All this was conveyed to me so that I should explore the issues further.

Some Specific Points of Disagreement

The EVP contested Manoj's understanding of the situation, particularly as described below:

- Though there were setbacks such as the lulls in the CMG meetings, it did put the CMG back on the rails. That was the time when Manoj had started his work and he helped us in the process of strengthening the CMG. However, it is not correct on his part to claim full credit for this.

- Manoj has described Ekta as a highly centralised organisation. But even when the founder was alive, there was considerable decentralisation. It is a misrepresentation because no central control is exercised over state-level operations of Ekta, and within the states considerable freedom and authority is provided for the various programmes.
- The basic OD intervention had touched only about 30 per cent of the staff and therefore Manoj should not have made generalised statements.
- That Ekta is a hierarchical organisation is partly true. The scale of operations requires some administrative hierarchy. However, there is considerable flexibility and leeway available within the programmes and one's direct responsibility areas, with relative ease of access to any level within Ekta. Policies are made in consultation, and there is consensus among the top management members.
- As regards systems, these were put in place during the founder's lifetime and we ensure that these systems are honed periodically as required.
- Manoj's identification of financial viability as the major *sutra* to move Ekta is most vigorously contested. 'This has been the most erroneous and the most damaging interpretation by the HR consultant. He failed to note that the bonding among the team members and the inner drive for their involvement do not come from financial viability considerations but from something else. These things were never identified and used for building up the HR initiative. The undue focus on financial viability as the justification for the change agenda only worked to erode the spirit and latent strength of human resources in Ekta.'

The Source of Discord

Even after these statements I realised that there was something more to it. It emerged as we were nearly closing our conversation. Mr Tandon felt that Manoj had become an 'extra constitutional authority' in the course of his work with Ekta. 'I can understand if he had to play the role of *Narad Muni* for the limited purpose of getting inputs for his facilitation. But his doing so, in the manner the legendary *muni* did, by instigating one against the other, was not at all correct. Many people here did not like this behaviour of his.' He concluded that, 'One would therefore need to question whether HR processes should be allowed to be spearheaded by outside consultants who have little accountability for organisational performance and commitments,' and whether an external HR consultant should be given a leeway to dabble in OD issues.

My Observations on Communication Styles in Ekta

After one-to-one discussions with juniors at the central research station, I had an opportunity to interact with about 25 junior, middle and senior level members in a large group. I found that the facial expressions of many indicated an eagerness to speak but they were doing so only after seeking approval of seniors present in a very imperceptible fashion. I jocularly remarked that members were not being open with me because every time permission had to be 'facially' conveyed–then the clarification came from the seniors that no junior need be afraid of speaking freely to me. Thereafter two members spoke about the diversity of work in the organisation.

Both at the formal meetings and in the field I noticed that it was the seniors who did most of the communicating. Also, it was the seniors who generated most of the ideas. Interestingly, when I asked several people at the organisation, (other than seniors), about the OD intervention, they said that they found Manoj always communicating only with the seniors and they wondered whether he was part of the senior management of the organisation.

There are issues, such as lesser pay packets for some juniors, which are discussed among them quite freely; however, none of them feels bold enough to raise this issue in a forum of discussion in the organisation. When I asked, 'Why are you then continuing to work in the organisation?' the reasons given were: proximity to native place, diversity of work and a strong loyalty to the ideals of the founder. There is thus some truth in Manoj's assessment of the need for financial stability within the organisation.

Conclusions

Harking back to the change process the EVP conceded that within the HR/OD ambit Manoj performed a 'variety of roles'–he was a process facilitator, sometimes a counsellor and at other times an expert. Going by the account that the MDP was highly successful, his role as a trainer obviously left a very positive impact. To me it appeared that Ekta, in keeping with its techno-managerial traditions, preferred to accept Manoj as an 'expert' in training rather than a consultant for their whole system.

The lesson here is obviously that the facilitator cannot afford to over-do any role, and must constantly carry out a reality check with the client. Sometimes a well-meaning effort could come out as something else. Manoj succeeded in making the seniors in Ekta keenly aware of the need for leadership development and the result was the MDP which earned a lot of positive feedback. His multiple role-playing, even as the change effort was on, led to complications.

Mr Tandon was open enough to tell me in the meeting that not having many thinkers is a weakness in Ekta, that it is mostly the seniors who do the idea-generation exercise, that there has to be more quality in work. This is definitely corroborating what Manoj said about the organisation at the end of the OD effort–'Ekta has become more aware of its characteristics without being defensive'. I would construe it as a positive fallout of the OD effort.

For me the most important lesson was that the communication process has to be very open and continuous. Both the client and the consultant must keep giving feedback to each other so that misunderstandings are sorted out in time. Nothing can be taken for granted.

I also recognised the challenges of building and maintaining the role boundary of a facilitator, especially when the system itself is ambivalent about its change agenda. There was a danger of the facilitator getting sucked into the power dynamics of the organisation. The intervention activity being distributed over four years, a very long time for someone to remain 'neutral', and the vulnerability of the facilitator in the face of such internal resistance, is another complex theme for reflection.

OD Tools and Techniques

(Based on the Formal Documentation)

Ekta 2010 Meeting

This was the initial diagnostic exploration in the OD process. It was felt that sustainable OD effort should emerge out of envisioning a preferred future and exploration of choices by a participatory process, involving significant role holders of Ekta. This forum was envisaged as a gathering of all CMG members and a cross section of executives across various locations, projects, sister organisations, levels of hierarchy and age groups. The meeting was conducted in July 2002 for six days and was designed on the large scale interactive process (LSIP) model.

Twenty-three members from the organisation participated and four members, including the consultant, anchored the process. Almost four days were spent in developing a shared understanding on the various issues.

The objectives of the meeting were:

- To understand the emerging trends in the development sector.
- To envision a preferred future for Ekta Development Research Foundation.
- To make choices–to take action today, to see the effects over the next three years.

To achieve these objectives, the meeting intended to brainstorm and decide about strategic directions for the coming years within the overall framework of the mission statement and shared values of Ekta, to look at an intermediate time frame, which will give opportunity to take actions and to renew Ekta in the next two to three years.

The various themes discussed during the meeting were as follows:

- Perspectives of different stakeholders of Ekta and their emerging trends.
- Mapping the psycho-social universe of the participants.
- Critique of major programmes of Ekta.
- Processing of issues and prioritising.

Table 3.1 Analysis of Tools and Techniques—Ekta *(Based on the Formal Documentation)*

Activity	*Methodology/Tools*	*Impact/Outcome*
	Entry	
	Recognition of Internal Needs and Invitation to Manoj	
	Diagnosis (6 days)	
Ekta 2010	LSIP–LSIP Tools, group work, the Existential Universal Mapper (EUM)	Recognition of personal emotional anchoring, critiquing of existing work–feedback in a non threatening way–a set of people committed to this change is formed, identifying vision and choosing strategy, reaffirming commitment to the organisation and feeling connected with it, identifying the most relevant issues, a stated vision and a course forward
	Interventions and Actions (spread across 4 years)	
Role clarity and transformation of EC and CMG meetings	Group work, group discussions, creating sub-committees for different themes	Engaged in self-reflective processes like using the IDRC organisational effectiveness framework, emerged as forums for learning best practices and develop new themes, and decentralisation manual amended

(*Table 3.1 continued*)

(*Table 3.1 continued*)

Activity	*Methodology/Tools*	*Impact/Outcome*
Development Centres	Identifying distinguishing competencies, assessing a cohort DC methods such as case studies on decision making, negotiation skills through role plays, GDs	An individual objective assessment of capabilities, peer group becomes aware of each others' qualities, resource pool identified within the organisation, participating in the assessment and dealing with 'expert' feedback and leadership potential identified for further grooming
HRM systems and manuals	Participatory process	Elimination of *ad hoc* decisions, brought focus to assessment and judicious decision-making
Campus Recruitment and Induction Processes		
MDP	Experiential activities for managerial skills and leadership, yoga, reading, learning diary, assignments	Individual strengthening of core abilities, mutual regard and learning, skills about managerial functions like finance, human resources, and so on. The CMG went through it first, accepted its value and then used it for others. Soft skills also acknowledged as important along with technical skills, shaping talent to suit needs preparation for further delegation
360-degree feedback and performance appraisal	Tried but not institutionalised	
Exit		
Pressure on consultant to move into the organisation, to head HR. Consultants choice to remain external eventually led to dissonance between the consultant and the EVP.		

The first three themes were interwoven in different sessions.

A series of small thematic presentations, by internal and external resource persons brought out the strengths, weaknesses, opportunities and threats (SWOT) of Ekta. The speakers included eminent persons representing different stakeholders such as a senior IAS officer, heads of reputed NGOs, an eminent economist, an advisor from the European Union India office, a business leader, a leading politician and a retired vice president of Ekta. Views of employees were ascertained through two quick surveys.

Three discussion papers were also presented by senior members of the CMG on the key activities of Ekta. The speakers were not directly involved with the subject matter they presented. This helped in getting a detached critique of the programmes.

These presentations helped in bringing out the achievements, joys and sorrows of the past, and hopes, fears and challenges for the future.

The key factors identified were:

(*i*) Centralised design and decentralised implementation.
(*ii*) Strong research base.
(*iii*) Technical and managerial manpower at headquarters and extension-oriented manpower at field.

It was decided that the OD effort would focus on enhancing these strengths.

'The Existential Universe Mapper (EUM)', an instrument developed by Mr Ashok Malhotra, a leading OD consultant, was used to understand the psycho-social universe of the entire group. This instrument is based on Clare Graves' 'Emergent Cyclical Levels of Existence Theory' (Graves 2001), an open system theory of values, with an evolutionary perspective of man. The instrument gives scores of six stages of evolution–mechanistic, individualistic, conformistic, aspirational, humanistic and holistic.

Development Centres

The main steps in this event were:

- Identifying and defining the competencies.
- Developing exercises to be used in DC for Ekta.
- Piloting the DC design with CMG members acting as participants.
- Identifying and training of assessors in and outside Ekta and to arrange the pool of skilled assessors.
- Refinement of competency descriptions and exercises based on CMG feedback.
- Conducting DC.
- Giving feedback to participants.
- Understanding the trend and preparing plan of action for development of competencies.

The following are certain highlights of the DCs.

Behavioural Science Centre (BSC) and Ekta had to design almost all the exercises used in the DC. For designing the exercises, lots of internal sources were tapped. A few cases from Kanitkar (1995) were adapted.

The exercises were of three types, as follows:

- Individual exercises (take decisions, develop proposals, or prepare a document or letter).
- Pair exercises (for negotiations–role-plays).
- Group exercises (discussions with other members).

Each DC had eight participants and two such groups underwent DC exercises at a given time, with a total of four assessors per group, (two internal and two external). Each competency was observed through two individual and two group exercises. All the eight group exercises were spread over three days to avoid monotony. Apart from these exercises designed for DC, a few other psychological instruments and questionnaires were also used. The purpose behind incorporating these instruments was to gain an overall picture of the person in order to facilitate the development process of the individual. Before the final interview the participants rated themselves, and these rating figures were used more as tools of conformation rather than assessment.

HR executives, academicians and counsellors from the industry were requested to volunteer as assessors. In return Ekta offered them training. The strategy worked. Internal assessors were drawn from a group of CMG members and other senior executives. Thus, half the assessors were internal and the other half were external.

The feedback was given to participants in two steps. First, feedback was given in-groups–sharing with the participants the method of arriving at the final score, its meaning, and so on. Second, individual meetings were scheduled with the concerned authorities and the participant, in which each person debated his scores. The consultant shared the behaviour in the DC, and the superiors shared their day-to-day experiences with respect to competencies. This design of feedback not only helped in creating an open mindset to work with oneself but also assured the candidate about the scope of development. In the end, specific action plans for improving the competencies were discussed and prepared.

Management Development Programmes

Objectives of the Management Development Programme were:

- To enhance the seven identified competencies,
- To increase knowledge and skills of managerial functions like HRD, finance, and so on,

- To encourage participants to discover the strength in themselves and others, and
- To provide an opportunity for learning from one another and developing relationships across Societies.

In all, 36 participants from various societies attended the programme. The participants were divided into two groups. There were two phases of fifteen day each for both the groups. The sessions were held from 9.30 am to 5.30 pm, followed by an hour of yoga at 6.15 pm. Every day the participants were required to do some reading, or work on a case or live issue facing them. On a few days the participants reported working up to 11.30 pm. In spite of this demanding schedule, their class participation was very enthusiastic. Each participant maintained a learning diary, in which he recorded what he/she learnt every day. These entries were not so much on the topics covered, but about the churning inside the mind, arising out of the various learning experiences. Most of the resource persons were familiar with development sector in general and Ekta in particular. Sessions taken by Ekta vice presidents were highly motivating for the participants as they could relate many of the concepts with their experiences. Similarly, actual issues were taken up for discussion in the classroom. These discussions helped participants to learn from one another.

Participants were given three assignments to be completed before the next phase. The enthusiasm and involvement of participants were very encouraging. The programme provided confidence to the top managers that adequate talent was available within to take up field management responsibilities. Along with the training many of the participants were also given larger responsibilities that helped them to practice what they learned. The second level of delegation of power was approved by the CMG, and this further helped the participants to exercise the necessary authority in taking operational decisions. The programme helped in bringing to the surface a lot of hidden and untapped potential of the participants.

REFERENCES

Graves, C.W. 2001. *ECLET-Emergent Cyclical Levels of Existence Theory* (14 audio cassettes). Santa Barbara, CA: ECLET Publishing.

Kanitkar, A. 1995. *Managerial Decision-making in Agricultural Cooperatives: Some Selected Cases.* New Delhi: International Cooperative Alliance.

Mouton, J.S. and R.R. Blake. 1984. *Synergogy: A New Strategy for Education, Training, and Development.* Austin, Tx: Scientific Methods, Inc.

4

Case II—Chaturya

An Experiment in Collective Leadership*

A Case Study Prepared under the C-POD Project for SRTT

The Context and the Institutions Involved
(Compiled by the C-POD Team)

Chaturya is a voluntary development organisation working since 1984 to protect, defend and promote the human rights of marginalised groups. Chaturya works with urban, rural and tribal communities in western India, on the issues of poverty, governance and environment.

The organisation had always practised participatory decision-making, so there was a culture of inclusion that was legitimised. However, in the first ten years of its existence, leadership and direction was provided mostly by the founder-CEO, who was looked up to as the ultimate arbitrator of all conflicts, the one who would take the final call on the way forward, after listening to diverse viewpoints. As a single, large and growing organisation, the responsibility for decision-making had slowly started to get decentralised since the mid-1990s.

---

* The intervention process was conducted during September 2003 to February 2004. The review was conducted in December 2006.

The late 1990s saw Chaturya reconstitute itself into four different sister entities–urban, rural, consulting and resource centre. This was done with the purpose of both widening Chaturya's outreach and simultaneously deepening its impact. At the same time, the founder-CEO expressed a desire to withdraw from that role, believing that it was time for him to move on, and also time for Chaturya to have someone new. Due to a variety of reasons, the newly constituted entities, barring Chaturya Rural, had as leaders people who had joined the organisation around the time of the restructuring process, or later. With a successor to the outgoing CEO proving elusive, the governing board decided to try a model of collective leadership–all four heads of the four entities coming together as the newly constituted senior management team (SMT) to collectively steer Chaturya in the interim. It was in the context of facilitating this transition from a CEO-led organisation to one that is managed by a collective leadership process that Synergies Consultants were called in.

Synergies, an organisation development and behavioural training firm that specialises in team-building and leadership development work, had previously done some short-term work with Chaturya, and since that experience had been positive, they were invited to facilitate the transition to collective leadership. The fact that the outgoing CEO personally knew Lokesh, one of the consultants from Synergies, may have been an added reason for his choice.

The Collective Leadership intervention was delivered through three workshops between September 2003 and February 2004. In December 2006 a reviewer, an OD consultant himself, interviewed some key participants in that intervention to get a sense of what that intervention meant to Chaturya then, and subsequently.

The OD Process and Event Structure

(Based on the Formal Documentation)

Steps in the Collective Leadership Intervention

Given that there had been no formal spaces where the outgoing CEO and the new SMT members had discussed the proposed collective leadership model, the first workshop was planned as an exploratory space where the SMT members and the others in leadership roles came together to face the reality of their having to lead the organisation without a CEO. The main outcome, as agreed between the CEO and the consultants, was to get the group to a point of emotional readiness for what lay ahead. Accordingly the workshop had as participants the outgoing CEO, the newly constituted SMT and a few others, who in the organisation's view, had a strong sense of what Chaturya, as an institution stood for. This workshop was of three-day duration.

Figure 4.1 Organisational Structure of Chaturya

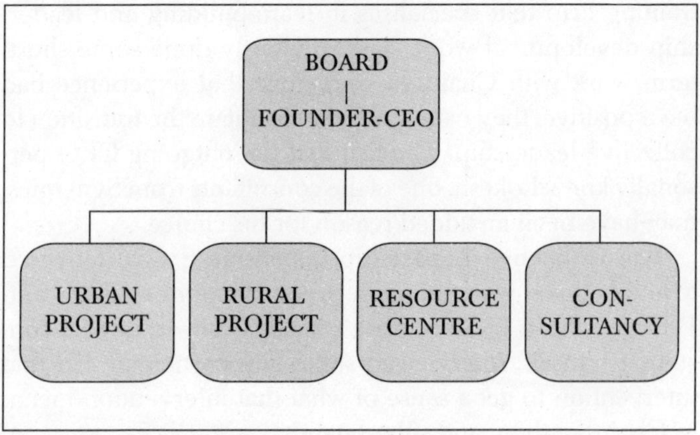

BOARD
|
FOUNDER-CEO

URBAN PROJECT
RURAL PROJECT
RESOURCE CENTRE
CON-SULTANCY

Figure 4.2 Steps in Collective Leadership Intervention

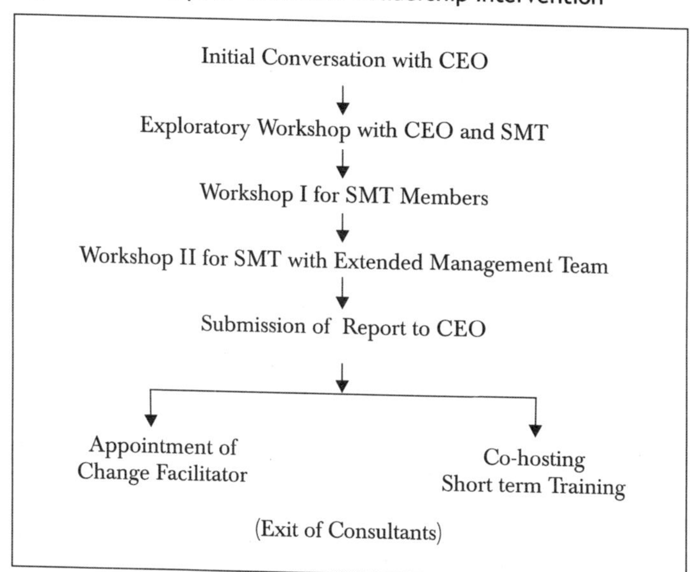

The First Workshop: Stepping into the Future

Workshop Objectives

- To provide an opportunity for the entity heads to face their anxieties and concerns about taking charge of collective leadership without a designated CEO.
- To enable the leaders to come together as a group on an emotional platform.
- To enhance their awareness and skills on leadership, particularly the aspects of managing their immediate and larger responsibilities simultaneously, and their ability to deal with uncertainty/ambiguity.
- To increase their comfort levels with risk-taking.

Significant Processes in the Workshop

The workshop was in many ways a landmark event in the life of the organisation, as never before had the senior management faced the prospect of their having to take charge. The participants in the workshop used that space constructively, building a better sense of bonding with one another, and articulating their concerns about steering Chaturya collectively. The first day was about anxiety about the future, and the second day was about a more realistic appraisal of both the strengths and weaknesses of the leadership group.

At the end of the second day, the outgoing CEO exited the workshop, due to prior commitments. For the consultants it was a revelation to watch how the group decided to take charge without the CEO on day three. In the toughest experiential outdoor activity in the workshop, at a critical juncture where moving forward seemed very difficult, the group made the decision of finishing the task.

Having articulated their fears and anxieties publicly, the group had by day three, realised their own leadership potentials–individual and collective. The result was that the members were less anxious and more excited about the future of their organisation.

Outcomes

- Members articulated their fears of taking Chaturya forward without the current CEO.
- Members realised their own leadership potential, individually and as a group.
- Members recognised their strengths and blocks as leaders, with the help of feedback from others.

At the end of the workshop, the group had a more realistic sense of both their strengths and weaknesses. They knew that they didn't have all the answers, but they also knew they could draw on the experience of one another in the leadership team and that of the governing board. Psychologically, the group had moved from a 'fear of failure' orientation to a 'hope of success' orientation about the impending change.

The Second Workshop: Towards Collective Leadership 1 (for SMT)

Having sensed that there were issues of competition, rivalry, and interpersonal trust among the members of the SMT that needed to be brought to the surface and dealt with, the consultants proposed a second workshop involving only the four SMT members who were directly in charge of the four entities of Chaturya. The SMT members also articulated the need for a dialogue amongst themselves on what collective leadership was all about. Accordingly, the consultants designed a second workshop exclusively for the SMT members.

Workshop Objectives

- Exploring and dealing with issues of transparency and openness; confrontation and caring; and responsibility and accountability amongst the SMT members.
- Working on enhancing the values of trust, faith, and confidence in each other as a team to lead the organisation into the future.
- Building a common understanding on what collective leadership was and how it could succeed within Chaturya.

Significant Processes in the Workshop

The SMT members came to the workshop with some apprehensions. With just the four of them in the same room for three days, and the unstructured methodology of the workshop that was proposed by the consultants and accepted by the group, it was probably inevitable that issues amongst themselves–feelings about each other's capability and style of leadership and instances of interpersonal misunderstanding from the past, would come out in the open and have to be dealt with. But they showed remarkable courage in designing the three-day workshop with the support of the consultants. Day one was about sharing perceptions about one another, day two was about a dialogue on the strengths and weaknesses of each SMT member, and day three was on concretising an action plan on how they would support each other to succeed as a collective. Some significant moments of the workshop which stood out in the minds of the consultants were:

- The courage the members showed in the pictorial representations of each other they made based on their perceptions of each other and the subsequent dialogue they had on why those images came to their minds about one another.
- The trust that developed between them as a group after the difficult sharing of each other's perceptions. One indicator of the trust was that members were open about their 'here and now' feelings with each other. They allowed themselves to be vulnerable and showed their anger, hurt, and tears publicly. The second indicator of the trust was that they did not avoid the conflict that such openness would engender; they showed the ability to stay with issues being unresolved for the moment.
- The generosity with which they listed the strengths that each of them brought forth after the first one and a half

days of dealing with issues of trust and accountability between them. The total picture that emerged of the strengths of each one of them was impressive. It was a moment where the group moved beyond the need to have an omnipotent and omniscient leader and accepted the strength of the collective.

- Day three saw an interactive session being conducted between the SMT members and the CEO of another NGO. Incidentally, this NGO had also gone through a similar collective leadership phase, and the SMT members benefited from the CEO's experiences of the challenges and triumphs of collective leadership. It was an honest and dispassionate message of great hope and it was important that the SMT members hear it at that point of time.

Outcomes

In the words of the SMT members themselves, some important outcomes of this workshop were:

- Discussing some past issues that had contributed to a climate of distrust and rivalry among them.
- Acknowledging each other's strengths and thus the strength of the collective.
- Acknowledging a significant sense of bonding among SMT members, and the commitment to support each other.
- Understanding the struggles and successes of collective leadership in another NGO and drawing hope from their experience.
- Developing some action plans on how SMT members could build each other's credibility within the organisation.

- Leaving behind the feeling of resentment towards the new leadership role during the course of the workshop and viewing the role as an opportunity for them to grow as leaders and influence the future of Chaturya.

Just after the workshop, the consultants witnessed an incident to show how the workshop impacted the SMT members. At the end of the workshop, the group decided to stay together and celebrate their new beginning with a dinner. One of the entity heads was scheduled to leave by train and would miss the dinner. Not wanting the sense of collectiveness to be disrupted, another entity head said she would release money for his air travel from her travel budget so that he could stay back and travel the next day. Given the history of competition between these two entity heads, this was no small step in the life of the SMT. The first entity head, who publicly acknowledged his gratitude, accepted the offer.

The Third Workshop: Broadening the Collective—Workshop with Extended Management Team

After the completion of the second workshop, where the SMT members moved forward on owning their role as collective leaders, the consultants proposed that they share this vision of collective leadership with their own second-line leaders, and enlist their commitment to supporting the SMT. This workshop was conceived as one that would be driven and led by the SMT members primarily, so that the rest of the extended management team in Chaturya started experiencing the collective leadership of the SMT in the workshop itself. It was agreed that the consultants would only support the SMT and the others members in engaging in a dialogue with each other.

Workshop Objectives

- To create a forum where the SMT could hear the concerns and anxieties of their own second-line leaders about the collective leadership process in Chaturya and also share their own perspectives and feelings about collective leadership.
- To create a space for the rest of the management team to articulate their expectations of the SMT and for the SMT to share their expectations.
- To enable the members to arrive at a point of personal commitment towards helping the collective to succeed.

Significant Processes in the Workshop

For the consultants, this was the toughest part of the OD process where they had to walk the tight-rope between enabling the SMT members take on the leadership role, while also enabling the rest of the leadership to articulate their perceptions, fears, and concerns about the very same SMT members. It was a chaotic workshop in many ways, with all participants including the consultants swimming in unknown waters, not quite knowing where they were headed.

The SMT members did a valiant job of listening carefully to the experiences of others about their own leadership styles as individual entity heads. Sometimes they accepted their faults and at other times defended their style and decisions. At a few critical moments in the workshop, they took charge of their role and confronted either an individual member or a group. What was particularly tough for the SMT members was to recognise that quite a few members in the second-line leadership carried a huge sense of disempowerment, and were stuck in a feeling of being exploited.

The consultants worked with the SMT members to help them accept the truth of the other members' experience of leadership styles in Chaturya. They confronted the second-line leadership with the implications of their own leadership behaviours. They also pointed out how they were delegating their issues on to others in Chaturya'.

Outcomes

- Dealing with the feelings of resistance/scepticism/apprehension among the management team members about the whole concept of collective leadership as well as its process in Chaturya in the new situation.
- Developing a deeper sense of interrelatedness and openness between the larger management team and the SMT in the context of the new roles being taken on by the latter.
- Understanding, through sharing of individual experiences, the patterns existing in Chaturya of:
  - (*i*) lack of transparency and openness among each other,
  - (*ii*) the sense of tiredness and 'giving up' that many members reach, and the reasons for it, and
  - (*iii*) their own tendency to push all responsibility for the organisation's health to those in leadership roles.
- Taking individual responsibility for changing the above patterns by developing individual and group action plans.

In contrast to the first two workshops where the mood in the group was exuberant at the end, the conclusion of the third workshop saw the group in a quiet, introspective mood. The consultants felt that the group was grappling with the enormity of what lay ahead in terms of the changes that are needed for transition of Chaturya into a genuinely shared leadership model.

Consultants' Report Submitted to the Outgoing CEO and SMT

After the third workshop the consultants summarised, in a report to the CEO and the SMT members, what the three workshops had together meant for the organisation.

- Recognition by the participants of the dangers of an entity-specific world view for the collective health of Chaturya.
- Realisation that one needs to hold both the entity identity and the larger organisational perspective together, for collective leadership to work.
- A sense of optimism and confidence about the new form of collective leadership.
- Understanding what is realistically possible to achieve through the collective leadership.
- Dialogue and shared understanding on:
  - (*i*) the strengths and weaknesses of Chaturya leadership,
  - (*ii*) what can help the collective leadership to succeed,
  - (*iii*) the need for a culture of nurturance, in order to be much more effective while engaging in the external work of Chaturya,
  - (*iv*) the need to balance the pace of expansion with spaces for people development,
  - (*v*) the need for much more transparency within the organisation, and
  - (*vi*) the need to build, rather than break, each other's leadership.

In the report, the consultants also flagged the following as critical leadership issues that required the attention and active support of the governing board if the SMT were to succeed as a collective:

- The need for detailing out specific roles, responsibilities, and authority of both the SMT and the larger management team in the context of collective leadership.
- The need for continuous support to the SMT to help them shift their role from managerial to leadership perspective.
- The need to take a closer look at the linkages between organisational strategy, systems and processes, and their impact on people's energy, passion, and commitment over a period of time.

Unplanned Exit of Consultants

As it turned out, this was the end of the engagement of the consultants with Chaturya's transition to collective leadership. They were not invited again for a dialogue, and their offer to share the experiences and perspectives with the board was not taken up, partly because there was a new change manager appointed by the governing board with the specific mandate of working with the SMT on an ongoing basis. But the consultants believe that it was also in part caused by the system's need to protect itself by 'gaining control' as a reaction to having exposed too much of its vulnerability, particularly in the last workshop.

One way in which the consultants' exit was managed by the client system without really calling it an exit, was that the organisation and the consultants' firm started work on co-hosting another short-term training programme. Caught in the details of this new and obviously exciting collaboration, it took the consultants a while to figure out that Chaturya did not need their services in steering the collective leadership process.

Reflections of the Consultants

Lokesh, one of the consultants from Synergies, stated:

> I gratefully acknowledge the contribution of my colleague Priya, who partnered me in all the stages of this intervention. While the words are mine, the thoughts and insights belong to both of us. I would also like to thank all the members who attended the C-POD II conference in February 2007, for their valuable and constructive feedback that has made this paper richer.

The Process of Entry

I saw Priya's as well as my entry as a result of my personal connection with the outgoing CEO of Chaturya (my wife had previously held a senior position in that organisation). While this was undoubtedly true to an extent, what this perception overlooked was that the competence and experience of both Priya and myself was thoroughly evaluated by a team of second-line managers in a face-to-face meeting. Despite this, I continued to see the CEO as the final authority, probably mirroring the reality of the client system at that point. It was also the year when both Priya and I were battling with our own fears of taking charge of Synergies as the founder and senior partner had gone on a sabbatical. The effect of this unconscious mirroring by us was that we continued to feel obliged to the CEO for having invited us to work with Chaturya, failing to hold in mind that the collective competence of our consulting firm was an important determinant of Chaturya's ultimate choice.

The fall-out of this position on Priya was significant, making her unusually tentative and reticent in our first meeting with the CEO. That the meeting happened at my residence instead of the formal office of Synergies only reinforced that perception of personal connection more strongly, making it even tougher for the entry of Priya as an equal. In hindsight, this blurring of the personal-professional boundary in our minds certainly made us more anxious, and probably built up anxieties in the client system too, about our competence.

But better sense soon prevailed as we started designing the first intervention where the inputs of all participants on the objectives of the workshop would be invited with the help of a questionnaire. The responses to the questionnaire made us realise the collective strength of Chaturya and helped us to go beyond dependence on the CEO. As we started the first workshop, we were much more in touch with our individual and collective competence.

Clarity on Who is Our Client

Perhaps this latching on to the CEO had made us believe that he was our client, whereas objectively, he couldn't have been, given that the intervention was about helping the organisation deal with the leadership question without him! In retrospect, it looked as if we had made the mistake of not getting clarity on who our client was in the organisation. Was it the outgoing CEO who called us in? Was it the board that mandated a collective leadership process for the organisation? Or was it the SMT which was expected to take charge of the leadership? We seemed to have behaved as if the outgoing CEO was our client in the first stage, and subsequently the SMT was our client, unwittingly ignoring other stakeholders in the system.

Linkages with All Stakeholders

Another lesson that we learnt was that while engaging in an OD intervention during a situation of flux in the client system, we needed to build stronger linkages with the key stakeholders in the system. In this instance, it occurred to us in hindsight that we were too focussed on the target audience of the intervention, to the exclusion of linkages with all other key players, such as the governing board. This may have made us more aware of what our intervention could be triggering off for the whole system and also corrected our pace. A better consulting practice required that we had a more holistic perspective of the total system even as we were engaging specifically with one part of the system.

Setting Boundaries to Engaging with a Particular System

Looking back, it seems like we made a mistake in getting into a parallel project with Chaturya, even as the SMT collective leadership intervention was going on. This led to a diffusion of focus, so much so that we were not aware of our role in the SMT intervention being quietly wound up! As mentioned earlier, it only seems to have made it easy for the client system to eject us out of that intervention, without the inconvenience of having any dialogue about it. Caught in our own need to grow, and feeling excited about the new training intervention that our consulting firm was offering the NGO sector along with Chaturya, we colluded in our own exit from the system. It would seem that a good consulting practice requires that the same consultants are not engaged in different projects with the same client system at the same time. We should have waited for the collective leadership intervention to come to a mutually agreed conclusion before starting on anything else.

Collective Leadership Three Years Hence

Impact Assessment of the OD Process by an External Reviewer

(By the C-POD Reviewer–2006)

Almost three years had lapsed between the intervention and its review. There were many organisational changes in the interim, and only a few members who were part of the collective leadership process were continuing in Chaturya. What was feasible for the reviewer was to have a telephonic conversation with the three persons who were part of the collective leadership intervention and were still playing key roles in the organisation. Based on the dialogue the reviewer had with these three people (two of them former members of the SMT), his understanding of the collective leadership OD intervention was as follows:

1. All three were appreciative of both the facilitators who were seen to be working in harmony.
2. The facilitators came across as professional individuals who were skilled in helping participants to come out with their feelings, not just facts or opinions. They were perceived as impartial and hence were able to confront issues.
3. The three workshops brought the participants closer as persons. They started becoming aware of the behaviour patterns of themselves and others, and were willing to seek more data before making up their minds about one another based on prejudices. At another level, they also became careful in expressing views lest the other person may become unhappy.

4. As an outcome of these meetings, one of the participants, on returning from a workshop, conducted a feedback session with her regional team. She mentioned that the session was helpful in getting the group closer.
5. In spite of these positives, the participants, over a period of time realised the futility of pursuing the 'collective leadership agenda'. They were able to perform their independent regional roles well, where they were the undisputed leaders. However, they could not fulfil the corporate responsibilities which they had divided amongst themselves, as collective leadership. Sometimes they found that their respective roles were demanding enough and hence could not spare adequate time for corporate responsibilities. At another level they found that they did not have adequate authority, and hence did not get adequate support from the other entities where they were not directly in charge of the operations. At yet another level, their aspirations, and competitive spirit, came in the way of cooperation. Over a period of time the SMT meetings became a drag. In the end, Chaturya was practically split into four entities and only certain functions of external compliances remained centralised.
6. The participants were critical of the role played by the board. They felt that the board was never convinced about the idea of collective leadership and hence this arrangement was seen as a stop-gap one till they found a new and competent CEO. Some of the participants felt that the board was possibly looking for one of the collective leadership members to emerge as the CEO, which continued the competition among the SMT members. The participants felt that the board had not involved them adequately. They felt that if only the board was involved in a similar process with

the same facilitators then things would have been different. The board members apparently had their internal deliberations with the help of some other facilitators.

7. At least two of the three participants felt that they had wasted their time in pursuing an unviable idea and they would not get into the 'collective leadership' mode again. Of the original four-member collective management team, two had left the organisation, and one was heading a separate campaign, on deputation from Chaturya.

OD Tools and Techniques

(Based on the Formal Documentation)

The First Workshop

At the very beginning of the intervention, the consultants designed an open-ended expectations form to collect some data from the people in leadership roles in Chaturya about what they thought needed to be the focus and outcomes of this OD intervention[1]. This form was useful in giving the consultants a more rounded view of the concerns and expectations of the organisation from this intervention, than the briefing they had received from the outgoing CEO. Moreover, it also brought home early in the intervention the collective competence that existed in the organisation.

Since both consultants were process-oriented trainers and believed in experiential learning as a methodology, the first workshop had a mix of structured experiential exercises and unstructured spaces for dialogue. This worked well,

Table 4.1 Analysis of Tools and Techniques—Chaturya *(Based on the Formal Documentation)*

Activity	*Methodology/Tools*	*Impact/Outcomes*
	Entry	
	Initial Conversation with CEO	
	Developing Contract	
Exploratory workshop with CEO and SMT (3 days)	Experiential learning through open-ended expectations form, structured activity with unstructured dialogue	Acknowledged fear to take on as leaders, recognised leadership potentials, explored strengths and weaknesses
	Design of Interventions	
Workshop 1 for SMT members (3 days)	Unstructured t-group: Interaction with CEO of another NGO	Dealt with past issues, developed sense of bonding and commitment towards each other, moved from viewing collective leadership as a burden to an opportunity

(*Table 4.1 continued*)

(*Table 4.1 continued*)

Activity	*Methodology/Tools*	*Impact/Outcomes*
	Assessing Impact	
Workshop 2 for SMT members with extended management team (3 days) Submission of Report to CEO	Hands-on experience with facilitation–SMTs as anchor persons	A sense of relatedness and openness between senior management and SMT, feelings of resistance, scepticism and apprehension emerged towards the change. Unplanned exit of the consultants by the appointment of a Change Manager
	Exit	
	Co-hosting short term training Appointment of change facilitator	

as the structured activities brought to the surface some dynamics about leadership styles, issues of competition, and rivalry which could then be linked to organisational patterns. Given that the group was coming together after a long time and was experiencing a high amount of anxiety, the structured activities also led to some thawing with each other and with the consultants, which made the dialogue spaces less threatening for all.

The Second Workshop

Dilemma on Methodology

With just four members as participants, the consultants faced the dilemma of whether only one of them should facilitate this intervention. Would two consultants be too much for a group of four to handle? The answers were not clear and the anxieties unresolved, but the consultants finally decided to work with the SMT group as a team of two, going by a hunch that the dynamics in this intervention were likely to be complex as all four SMT members were formidable leaders in their own right.

The second and more important dilemma was the methodology. While both the consultants believed that an unstructured T-group-like space was best suited for working on the objectives of the workshop (two SMT members had experienced T-groups earlier), there was concern about whether things would get too hot for members and consultants to handle, and whether an unstructured space would work in an organisational context; and whether the SMT members themselves would be comfortable with the proposed methodology.

A Consultative Process for Resolution of Dilemma

When the consultants checked with the SMT members on the first day of this intervention, they seemed willing to take the risk of working in an unstructured exploratory space. One of them pointed out that given all the ambiguities they have to face in their new role as the collective management of Chaturya, they might as well start facing it in the workshop! It turned out to be an instance where the consultants' trust in their and the participant group's judgement was validated. For the next two days, the SMT members worked with great courage on the issues of trust, transparency, competition, and mutual accountability amongst themselves.

Inviting a Third, External Resource Person

In the context of preparing the SMT members for their roles, the author thought of inviting the CEO of another NGO that had previously gone through the collective leadership phase, as guest speaker for an experience-sharing session. The main author had earlier worked in that NGO as HR manager at a time when that organisation was going through a phase of collective management, as part of the process of transition in leadership. The CEO of the NGO gladly accepted the invitation and agreed to an experience-sharing session with the Chaturya SMT as part of the second workshop. For a moment, the consultant grappled with the fear that he and his colleague would be outclassed by the guest speaker. Fortunately this anxiety was contained, and the session went ahead as scheduled.

It was a truly humbling moment for both the consultants to recognise the message of hope that the invited CEO conveyed to the SMT members of Chaturya. Her sharing of the strengths and pitfalls of the collective management phase in her own organisation, and her conviction that it was definitely useful for her NGO, went a long way in helping the SMT members see their new role as an opportunity instead of a burden imposed on them. In retrospect, the consultants remembered that session as a defining moment in the SMT's journey of collective leadership.

The Third Workshop

Transferring Ownership to the SMT Members

For the third (and last, as it turned out) phase of this intervention, the consultants believed that the SMT members' needed to play a key role in the delivery of the workshop. They needed to practise collective leadership in action, and what better place to start this than a workshop with their own immediate second line? They also needed to be seen by the rest of the organisation as having taken charge, if the organisation had to believe in the concept of collective leadership as viable.

So the workshop was differently designed. Each session had one SMT member as the main anchorperson, and another SMT member would support her/his role. The consultants largely played the part of coach/mentor to the SMT members backstage by helping them conduct a dialogue of their feelings about the facilitator's mantle they had donned, and enlarging their options of dealing with having a feeling of being 'stuck' in the group. At times it seemed like the workshop was going nowhere, but the consultants were able to resist their own temptation to take charge, and let the SMT members find their own creative ways out of what seemed a deadlock.

In the end, this stance of the consultants seemed to have worked well for both the SMT members, who displayed their leadership potential, and for the other members who had a chance to see their new leaders in action.

APPENDIX 4.1

Expectations Form

Participants are requested to complete this form and mail it to us after they have gone through the objectives of the workshop outlined by us. This will help us have a broader understanding of your own expectations from this intervention.

1. What outcomes do you expect for yourself and the leadership group at the end of this intervention?
   a.
   b.
   c.
   d.
2. What are your expectations from the facilitators of this intervention?
   a.
   b.
   c.
3. What are your expectations from other group members who are part of this intervention?
   a.
   b.
   c.
4. Any other concerns you may have

5

Case III—Prakruti

Gender Mainstreaming and Organisational Development*

A Case Study Prepared under the C-POD Project Supported by SRTT

The Context and the Institutions Involved
(Compiled by the C-POD Team)

Founded by a missionary in 1982, Prakruti focuses on building natural resources through a participatory watershed approach in a region severely affected by drought and poverty. Its activities include treatment of dry land, building water-harvesting structures, planting fruit trees, promoting rain-fed farming practices, constructing biogas units and smokeless *chullahs* through village organisations.

Prakruti, with the support of the state government is currently implementing 63 such watershed projects, in 15 mandals of a district. The organisation with a strong and committed leadership and 87 dedicated programme staff

* The intervention process was conducted during April 2002 to March 2006. The review was conducted in December 2006.

organised into four 'area teams' is well known for its socio-technical excellence, participatory processes, extensive coverage and intensity of work. The organisation has a staff-strength of 107, of which only six are women (three programme and three support staff).

Over the years the strategy and approach of Prakruti has evolved from implementation of soil and water conservation measures in lands belonging to Dalit farmers to developing a 'model village' with integrated watershed development. In this process of evolution, gender and equity along with institution building emerged as key issues, and the organisation became aware of the need to focus on gender along with social effectiveness.

Theme

The thematic focus of the intervention was on mainstreaming gender. Focus (the consultants for the gender mainstreaming process) believes that mainstreaming gender is much more than training programmes and building perspectives. The main challenge in mainstreaming is addressing gender in all the elements of the organisation and bringing gender-sensitive changes in programme activities, processes and culture of the said organisation. It is actually understanding and working, with thinking, feeling, and behavioural processes.

Keeping this in mind, both Focus and Prakruti recognised and agreed right at the beginning of the partnership that substantive changes in gender mainstreaming would, and should, lead to organisational development. With this understanding focus accompanied the planned change processes over a period of eighteen months. The project intervention was in the nature of an action-research project.

THE JOURNEY—REFLECTIONS OF THE FACILITATORS

First Contact

The request for support from Prakruti came through an associate of ours. We responded positively to the request in principle, as we were enthusiastic about mainstreaming gender with a large organisation engaged in natural resource management.

Before entering into a formal contract, we made a field visit to one of the project villages, followed by a meeting with the head of the organisation and a core group of staff members. During this meeting the following observations were made, which were accepted by the group:

- The organisation primarily showed a technical orientation in the implementation of the programme focusing on planned field activities.
- There was less participation of women in the community interaction.
- Female programme staff (six out of 107) were not clear about their role in the organisation.
- The male staff believed that gender has everything to do with women, so the female staff should handle it.
- The culture was hierarchical, as seen by the way the staff behaved in the presence of the leaders.
- The task orientation of the organisation meant that there was a gap between formal and informal communication in the organisation.
- The major concern was around the economic dimension of development and 'the increase in income levels'.

Terms of Reference

This initial interaction with the NGO gave us the impression that they were looking at 'adding on' gender in the on-going activities, which essentially meant including women. However, we were of the opinion that to bring in a lasting change, gender had to be mainstreamed internally in the organisation as well as externally in their programme activities. Gender did not only mean adding more women, but also promoting a new perspective of looking at gender holistically. Thus, the following critical elements of the partnership were jointly identified:

- As gender is organically linked to all aspects of organisational functioning it was agreed that gender needed to be addressed in the overall framework of organisational development.
- To facilitate effective learning it was important to focus on diverse processes and its interconnections operating both within the organisation as well as in the communities. Thus, a process-oriented, action-research approach was to be adopted from the beginning.
- A steering committee was to be formed to design and *operationalise* the intervention, along with Focus.
- The lessons from this partnership for mainstreaming gender and organisational development were to be documented for wider sharing.

Clarifying the understanding on gender and agreeing to these basic approaches at the entry and contracting stage contributed largely to the smooth planning and implementation phase of the project. An action-learning process was adopted wherein most of the interventions that followed were planned and built on the experiences of introducing gender in the organisation.

For the concept of gender used in the intervention process, see Appendix 5.1.

Diagnosis

After working with them for six months and developing an understanding of the organisation, we developed a hypothesis about the different aspects of the NGO as depicted in the diagram (see Figure 5.1). The diagrammatic representation captures the critical processes that operated in the organisation, and the major push-pull factors that influenced the attitude and behaviour of the organisation and the staff.

The inner circles represent the existing orientation built over a period of several years. Technology focus, task orientation, and enhancing economic productivity with a predominant association with men represent these primary aspects. The outer circles represent aspects given secondary importance within the organisation that needed to be addressed for mainstreaming gender. Thus, the challenge that we faced was also to promote a bi-polar approach in the organisational functioning and activities.

Design of Interventions

The interventions focused on all the areas identified in our diagnosis of the organisation.

We adopted a multi-dimensional approach to accompany this dynamic process. In planning our initial interventions, we kept in mind the change facilitation mantra attributed to Kurt Lewin, 'If you want to truly understand something, try to change it'. We were clear that we couldn't fully understand an organisation in the initial diagnosis. What was required was an accompaniment process based on action-research approach. The methodology comprised learning events,

Figure 5.1 The Changes Required—Inner and Outer

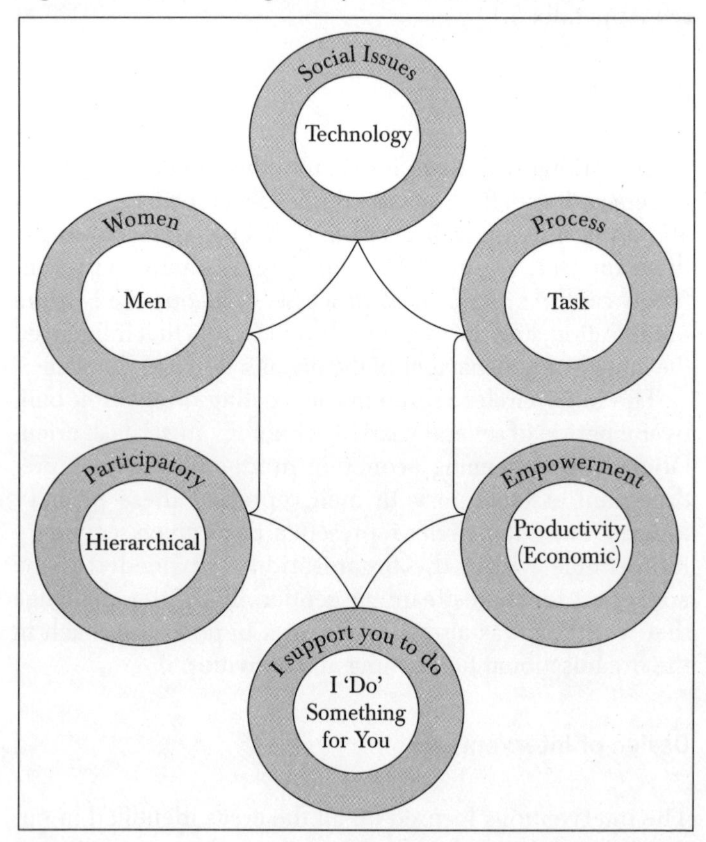

review meetings at different levels, field observation and feedback, capacity-building of women staff, and discussing with the leadership. In view of this the following steps were planned:

- Building gender perspectives at the core group and field staff levels.

- Building up competencies of the women staff.
- Integrating gender in watershed activities.
- Arranging periodic field visits for review, reflection, and action planning with area teams.
- Developing tools for gender training and building training skills of village-level staff.
- Arranging organisational-level review meetings.

In the entire process, we visualised our role as a 'fellow traveller' who was exploring problems together for mutual learning and not as a 'knower' and 'solution provider'. The diagram on accompaniment (Figure 5.1) will show the diverse elements that have to be addressed in the accompaniment process.

The collaboration of one and a half years can be broadly classified into two phases.

Phase I: 'Preparing the Ground'

The focus was on strengthening the internal learning environment and building gender perspectives. This phase that covered the first six months of work included two types of programmes.

Exploring People and Organisational Processes

Working on gender required a fair amount of ability to reflect and interact with others without being affected by age, position, or sex in order to be critical about self, others and the organisational processes. During the initial visits, we observed the strong hierarchical nature in the organisation and realised that strengthening internal learning processes among the staff of the organisation would be the very important first step.

To address this, a four-day learning event on 'Exploring People and Organisational Processes' was conducted for a group of 25 members in leadership positions. Designed as a precursor to the learning event on gender, the programme focused on enhancing the understanding on intra-personal, inter-personal, and group processes. The methodology included small, unstructured work groups; semi-structured exercises and input sessions. Recognising the value of the workshop, the organisation decided to extend the programme to its entire staff. In fact, the programme was repeated thrice. At the end of each session, action plans were prepared. Strengthening inter-personal relationships, communication, introducing feedback culture, and working towards consensus in decision-making were some of the main areas identified for planning action. These programmes also helped us to understand different issues at the organisational level, and to establish a rapport with all the staff.

Perspective Building on Gender for Core Group of the Organisation

A four-day workshop on building perspectives in gender was conducted wherein the core group of the organisation along with the director participated. The workshop focused on building awareness on gender construction in the self and society by examining gender positions in the organisation and identifying and initiating change processes towards mainstreaming gender in the organisation and in projects.

Phase II: 'Sowing the Seeds and Nurturing the Seedlings'

This phase of work included a number of multi-dimensional interventions.

Monthly Accompaniment Visits

To support the implementation of action plans and to further understand the organisational- and village-level gender issues monthly visits were made to all the four areas.

Box 5.1 Accompaniment Process

> Accompaniment is an approach to facilitate organisational change in social development organisations. It is essentially the facilitator walking with the organisation towards mutual learning in an effort to extend a learning environment beyond training hall situations. The accompaniment process performs the critical function of 'holding' the diverse learning processes of the organisation. Apart from building perspectives in a training hall situation, facilitating reflection spaces, joint planning, handholding and supporting individuals, and documenting the processes are the other major components of the accompaniment.
>
> The accompaniment process also helps understand that mainstreaming gender is linked to the way the organisation perceives natural resource management itself–resources that need to be 'managed' or resources which are a part of a holistic inter-connected ecology perspective. Gender is seen as an intrinsic part of the holistic ecology perspective.

Capacity-Building for Women Staff

A continuous process of dialoguing and reflecting with the women staff to share their experiences and build their confidence was attempted. In addition, a three-day event was organised in the campus. This event focused on knitting the women team together, exploring their roles based on the expectations of the other staff, and enhancing their understanding on gender and ecology.

This exercise gave the women clarity on their roles, their existing skills, and the skills that needed to be developed.

Review Meeting

A joint review of six months of the gender mainstreaming process was organised which included the entire core team and technical and executive directors. The meeting provided an opportunity to the area teams to share and reflect on the experiences–challenges and lessons related to the implementation of gender action plans.

Perspective Building on Gender for all Field Staff

A gender perspective programme in the local language was conducted for all the area teams. Here the emphasis was on gender in livelihoods and ecology with examples from the field level. Two women staff co-facilitated the programme which helped to enhance their facilitation skills and understanding on gender.

Enhancing Facilitation Skills

One of the areas of intervention identified during accompaniment was upgradation of the facilitation skills of the organisation. Therefore, in addition to in-house training, selected staff members were deputed for training outside. The female staff members were deputed to participate in moderation skills programme and four other staff members were deputed to participate in personal growth labs.

Developing Training Tools on Gender for Field Staff

In order to understand and learn from the field experiences of other successful initiatives on integrating gender in Prakruti, a woman leader involved in similar work was invited to interact with the staff.

Some of the Important Outcomes

- Recognisation of need: The need for mainstreaming gender had successfully percolated down to the various levels in the organisation, and had many gender advocates–both men and women. This we saw as one of the main achievements of this process.
- Change in culture: Monthly meetings of staff slowly started becoming informal. The earlier practice of reporting target achievements and rigid planning gave way to sharing experiences and discussing processes. This also provided space to bring out qualitative elements in the work. This in turn led to the staff at the middle level having a greater say in the decision-making process.
- Project intervention: The number of women participating in the watershed implementation programme went up. Women started taking on non-traditional roles such as taking measurements and monitoring the quality of land work. The organisation started planning interventions with both women and men, rather than attempting to integrate women into already planned interventions. Backyard horticulture and kitchen garden promotions proved successful examples in this regard. The wages earned by women were given to women, unlike the earlier practice of giving these to men. Initially, there was resistance from some villages but slowly this was accepted and appreciated. The organisation also made it compulsory to get the signature of women farmers on the agreements before taking up land development work. This move strengthened the identity of women

as farmers and recognised them as equal shareholders in the development of land.
- Feedback culture within the organisation: The feedback culture slowly took root in the organisation. This helped staff to share what they felt about the others in a non-judgemental way.
- The attitudinal change in male staff regarding gender was appreciable. Though they found it a challenge, many were going ahead with the agenda and in fact, motivating the women and field staff. In the area level, gender had become a point of discussion in the team meetings. The attempt at gender mainstreaming had increased the interaction of the male staff with the village women. The staff members themselves admitted that there was an increased interaction among men and women staff.
- The organisation was giving first priority to women candidates in matters of employment.
- Strategic orientation: At the end of this phase, the organisation also initiated a strategic re-orientation process. The gender-sensitive ecological perspective was kept central to evolve the strategic orientation of the organisation. The strategy to plan and implement interventions with the household as reference, instead of the village or watershed community, gave scope to recognise and integrate micro level gender issues into the project interventions.

Reflections and Lessons Learnt

Eighteen months is not an enormous period in the lifespan of a 23–year-old organisation, and this should be kept in mind when we talk about the gender mainstreaming process in an organisation that is entrenched in the cultural and developmental context of its parent organisation. But looking back we believe that it is extremely important to assess the shifts it has brought in and look at the issues for future focus.

To initiate and sustain organisational-level change processes, there is a need for some supporting factors within the organisation such as commitment of leadership, a critical mass in the organisation believing in the relevance of gender, and openness for change in the organisation.

It is obvious that gender requires a change in the culture, structures and programme strategy of the organisation. This process, however, has also brought certain questions in the very concept of watershed and how organisations are adopting it when you look at it from the gender lens.

Joys and Challenges

- One of the main factors that helped in our work was the woman/man team of consultants which demonstrated collaborative working styles.
- During the first few interactions, we felt we were struggling with a monolith, which had no emotional responses. Whatever we spoke was heard with a deadpan expression by most of the staff. We were seen as the authority brought in by the boss. So whatever we said was agreed upon in totality with no dialogue, confrontation, or understanding.
- After the initial programme on exploring self and group relations in which we used the T-group methodology (a methodology used to build sensitivity to human processes and group dynamics among the participants), there was some movement, especially when the staff saw that the senior-most people changed their behaviour. This loosening up of the atmosphere in the organisation paved the way for initiating dialogue on gender.

- The participation of one of the consultants in a programme on understanding unconscious processes was a turning point in our interventions. This particular project was used as a case for learning. It brought home the understanding that when natural resources were seen as resources to be 'managed', it was a very masculine stance and not an inter-connected, 'holding' nurturing feminine stance. Such a stance is built on the care-giving roles generally taken up by women and seen as feminine by the society at large.
- It was only after that that we brought in the holistic concept of ecology as an integrative framework looking at natural resources, gender, institutions, and community. From then on we felt the gestalt as to the place of gender in ecology was complete within us and therefore there was more acceptance in the organisation. Thus, this demonstrated to us how interconnected the learning of the facilitators and the partner-client organisation could be.
- This experience again confirmed our understanding that 'mainstreaming' gender was a much more complex and holistic process requiring organisational-level reflection leading to redesigning of frameworks. In comparison, organisations were more comfortable with 'integrating' gender, which had limited focus on 'adding on' to the existing programme frameworks.
- Our work with Prakruti also showed that an equal number of women and men in an organisation was desired but not absolutely necessary to evolve into a gender-sensitive organisation. We realised that mainstreaming gender was not only about achieving equality in numbers, but also about developing sensitivity and perspective.
- As in any OD intervention, for gender too, the sponsorship and the commitment of the leaders were very

important. The leader of Prakruti was aware of, involved in, and provided exceptional support during, the process of gender mainstreaming and responded positively to all the changes that it necessitated.
- When the organisation started a strategic re-orientation process, gender and ecology approaches became an integral part of the future strategy.

This experience brought home the fact that deep-seated changes in an organisation are possible and connected to the changes within the staff and the leaders. If change is seen as something to be done with others and in the activities, those changes will not be long-lasting and sustainable. One cannot sponsor change for others–*change can't be 'out-sourced'!*

Mainstreaming gender in an organisation demands attention towards many other aspects such as values, culture, perspectives, and programme management–usually considered outside the 'gender domain'. Convincing the leadership and the staff that gender is linked to all these activities of organisational function was a challenge.

Conclusion

Once the strategic re-orientation process was complete, this phase of our partnership with the organisation would come to an end. A lot had been achieved, yet a lot remained to be done–mainstreaming gender is a continuing process. The organisational staff had developed awareness and some sensitivity on the issue. However, being a natural resource management implementation organisation with donor funds, Prakruti's primary concern remains fulfilling the objectives of the projects. The organisation struggles to balance tasks and processes. As long as this and other dichotomies depicted earlier remain in a creative tension, there is hope for progress in mainstreaming gender in the organisation.

OD Methods—An Assessment

(By the C-POD Reviewer–November 2006)

The reviewer visited Prakruti, and met with its director, and members of a steering committee on 6 November 2006. They went through all the documents on the instruments developed for gender sensitivity available at the centre and Focus, and also the interactions between the OD consultant and the client.

Triggers for Process

Prakruti's activities (mainly watershed development) were aimed at improving the quality of resource base and access to local resources for the marginalised or excluded groups in the community. However, very few women ever came to these meetings or took any active interest in the watershed-related discussions, planning, or execution. Even when the field staff remembered to ask them, the response was that they were busy with their household activities. The women's self-help groups (SHGs) formed by Prakruti, were not structured to mobilise women for these projects. Therefore, aware of their focus and mandate, they initiated discussions with the consultants to mainstream gender in their field operations.

Gender Mainstreaming and its Connection with the Core Purpose

The lessons from the first set of watershed development projects across India indicated clearly that benefits are sustainable only when both men and women in the community are mobilised to participate in the planning and implementation of such projects. The leadership at Prakruti recognised the importance of this and wished to make necessary changes. Their efforts seemed to need 'something more', and this was when they called in a consultant. They were seeking a 'gender' consultant who would improve the gender balance in their programmes.

The Consulting Organisation

The consulting organisation they contacted was Focus, an NGO committed to a range of services in OD, HRM and change facilitation. The organisation's core purpose was to 'walk-along' with organisations, groups or individuals, in the social development sector as they managed personal and institutional transitions. The consultant's task therefore got shaped very differently. The gender-mainstreaming accompaniment was an effort to handle both internal and external imbalances between men and women, well ingrained in the social, economic, and political fabric. This meant that both men and women had to accept their contributions to this situation, and actively work towards a change. It was not a gender-strategy assignment where a consultant studied the working and made suggestions. Therefore, the consultants approached the issue in an holistic manner and an OD process involving both 'inside' and 'outside' elements became the vehicle for the change effort.

Stages in the Contracting Process

The shift that occurred in the initial phase was a redefining of the issues–from '*how do we get women to participate more*' to '*how do we deal with the prevailing norms about gender balance*' both within and outside the organisation. The design was shaped with mutual agreement and contributions.

The Steps in the OD Process

The Diagnosis

The diagnosis was presented to the client system in an elegant model and identified six elements–four relating to the output and external elements, and two pertaining to interactions amongst the people. It indicated the need for better integration, or balancing, between the polarities of these elements. The steering committee (as constituted) had varying levels of comfort with the different elements. It did not see itself as hierarchical and unemotional, or holding back direct expression of feelings. It also saw that the women within the organisation were well treated. The organisation had gone through an overall shift from Natural Resource Management (NRM) orientation to ecology and was as of then, on to livelihood. Their understanding of the issues changed once they recognised that Prakruti had to shift from the exploitation of a natural resource to an approach sensitive to balancing and respecting all living systems around the watershed.

At a recent meeting with the steering group there was hardly any acknowledgement of ecology or the way the gender mainstreaming process brought this up. Currently, the focus is on livelihood development with underlying implications that the resource would be used to optimise or sustain the benefits that humans can derive from the natural resource, rather than emphasising on natural balance or conservation. This is a pointer to the strength of the socio-technical orientation in the organisation and the level of integration of gender mainstreaming as a concept.

Stages in the Accompaniment Process

The various steps in the accompaniment process were discussed with the steering committee and all the staff members providing their inputs. The memories of these events were captured in the course of the discussions with the steering committee.

The group had a good recollection of the workshops on exploring self, interpersonal and organisational processes. The group felt that the workshops were quite conceptual to build gender perspectives but they were said to have had less of an impact because the staff was not able to absorb all the concepts shared very readily.

Sensitisation of Field Staff

The instrument used for gender sensitisation was remembered–it was acknowledged that it helped the staff to reorient themselves, especially in the fieldwork. This was identified as the most powerful step in the accompaniment process. Staff members became more conscious of the ways in which women got excluded. They began to make efforts to bring women to the meetings on watersheds. They have since made efforts to get both men and women to participate in watershed-based livelihood schemes with visible impact in the field. The watershed committees have almost equal number of women and men participating now. The inclusion of women in the project activities like bunding, tree planting and horticulture has reportedly led to better care for the plantations and improved monitoring of quality during construction.

Feedback from the Village

The discussions in one of the project villages revealed that these interventions have actually improved the living conditions in the village by creating employment and water resource availability. The watershed projects are implemented under the Hariyali guidelines and both men and women have equally benefited from the opportunities. The staff has now begun forming mixed work teams for bunding and levelling, and men and women are paid equal wages. The women are paid directly and have greater control over their earnings. Women are now playing a greater role in horticulture by learning about sprinklers, new crop varieties, and similar technical innovations. This has become possible because of a greater awareness and the desire among staff members to address gender imbalances. This is clearly a direct outcome of the combination of personal growth and training on gender perspectives imparted to the field staff.

Capacity-building for Women Staff

The women members of the steering committee spoke of the changes in the way they now work in the field. Women's groups in the community are no longer seen as the responsibility of women staff members alone. Serious effort has been made to increase the number of women working in the organisation and there is now an attempt to recruit more women than men. However there is no significant change in the number of women on the staff. There have been some new recruits, especially with technical expertise or in the office, but most have had to leave because of personal reasons like marriage and/or transfer of husbands. The area managers still feel that it is tough for women to work in remote locations and prefer to give them desk jobs. Thus, though there is more awareness and acceptance, there is little change in the outlook and mindset, leading to inadequate representation of women in the field teams in the project areas.

Documentation

Focus undertook to document the changes in the villages but the steering committee has not been able to see the documents. On the whole, the opinion was that the documentation was a bit intrusive and done without much concern for the convenience of the community or the field staff.

Impact on Structures, Systems and Processes

The Steering Committee

This structure was introduced during the accompaniment process and continues to work on the agenda even after the OD intervention, though the original composition of the steering committee has now changed with the exit of a few members. The change reflects the formalisation of the steering committee and its integration with the power structure and is no longer merely a unit of individuals largely concerned with gender imbalance. The area team leaders and two women are now on the committee. The issues pertaining to women's participation in watershed activities gets reviewed at the area and head office levels and the steering committee members invariably attend these reviews. The indicators tracked are the number of women members in each committee and the opportunities availed of by women in the various initiatives arising from the watershed programme.

Changes in Perceptions in the Village

The project staff have arranged for exposure visits and training for women in developing their SHGs, managing their thrift and credit transactions, and bank linkages. The women appreciate the care and thank the organisation that made these trips memorable events in their lives. They feel confident about managing their own affairs.

The village men have become more understanding to the pressures faced by women. They have realised how the women, in such a short span of time, gained the knowledge and confidence to collect savings service loans and deal directly with banks. The men have been inspired by the thrift and credit operations of their village women's groups so much that they have begun to form men's savings groups. They have been banking their savings for the last six months and will soon be eligible to take loans from the bank. The innovations and experiences in bringing women more directly into the circle of these activities could be seen as an indicator of mainstreaming at one level.

Attitude towards Women Staff Members

The organisation is quite protective towards its women staff members. Field placements are still seen as tough for them, and the women themselves too believe and accept this position. There has been some redesign of roles, especially of the men in the organisation, so that 'women's issues' in the field are not just left to the small minority of women staff actually working in the field. All women staff members get to meet the director every month and also an opportunity to share their experiences and learn about organisational priorities. This sometimes evokes some teasing among the male colleagues especially because it is rare for a junior male staff member in the project to meet the director. The women value the opportunity this provides for them to network with each other across the organisation. In general, the respect shown to women on the staff is high. Any report of misbehaviour with women staff is treated seriously and the issue goes right up to the top management. It helps that there are couples in the senior management team who head different projects and initiatives of the organisation.

Reviewer's Observations

The project demonstrates how social perspectives can be addressed through the OD intervention vehicle. It also illustrates the possibility of the consultant remaining an outsider while accompanying the change process. It offers important lessons for organisational change facilitators in the social development arena from both these perspectives.

It typifies the challenges of 'mainstreaming' or 'internalising' an overarching identity issue which is larger than the organisation itself, arising from the larger socio-cultural context. Other such issues could be caste, ethnicity or religion. Organisations perceive such issues gradually as they deepen their understanding of the challenges they face in enlarging and stabilising impact. This project therefore recognised the significance of gender disparities as a hindering factor and accepted the need to tackle such an issue only after a well-established track record of successful project implementation.

One stage in this transformation has been accomplished with the articulation of the need to deal with men and women in the community on equal terms. Ways of working in the field to ensure women's complete participation have been tried, tested and converted to standard practice in the project. These aspects have been integrated into the existing project planning, management and review processes and the steering committee continues to hold the focus on the issue steadily.

The other aspect of the challenge is to work on the gender dynamics within the organisation. Here the transition has been more difficult, and women in the organisation are still seen as protected. Given the small number of women staff, it is perhaps still possible to view them as 'exotic'. Prakruti still prefers to maintain status quo within the organisation. For the moment it seems content to look outward rather than inward. But once the organisation manages to recruit and retain larger number of women as field staff, it will have to contend with the challenge of building equality between men and women.

The lesson for the change facilitator then is to take the client system further down the road it wishes them to travel without pushing or forcing the pace. In an accompaniment process the partners walk together with goodwill and mutual respect up to the point they have agreed upon–and not to the journey's end.

OD Tools and Techniques

(Based on the Formal Documentation)

Our work at Prakruti gave us an opportunity to reflect and develop different approaches and helped us to gain conceptual clarity on the different themes involved in mainstreaming gender.

The process helped develop a framework for understanding gender and ecology. This framework can be referred to in understanding the interrelationships between different dimensions and crosscutting themes involved in mainstreaming gender in ecology. Questions can be raised on each dimension to explore the existing stances of the organisation.

A profile of a gender-sensitive organisation (see Appendix 5.2) was further developed, based on the work of the Royal Tropical Institute of Netherlands. This tool helps organisations to check the gender sensitivity and identify areas of work. This tool is also useful in understanding the priorities of the staff from different organisational levels. It is particularly helpful in initiating an in-depth discussion on gender culture of the organisation.

Table 5.1 Analysis of Tools and Techniques–Prakruti
(Based on the Formal Documentation)

Activity	*Methodology*	*Impact/Outcomes*
	Entry	
	First Contact through Associate	
	Developing the Contract	
Field visit followed by meeting		Very low involvement of women in water shed work
	Developing Terms of Reference *Interventions*	
Learning event I–exploring people and organisational processes (4 days)	Semi-structured activities and exercises on intra-/inter-personal communication, feedback, and so on	Self awareness and opening out to each other, set up greater communication, prepare them for gender workshops
Learning event II–perspective building on gender (4 days)	Experiential activities to reflect on gender issues in the personal organisational, and social spheres, to develop concept of gender and for gender profiling.	Recognising linking of gender within and without, recognising strategic significance of gender and ecology framework, prepared for further work

(*Table 5.1 continued*)

(*Table 5.1 continued*)

Activity	*Methodology*	*Impact/Outcomes*
Learning event III–perspective building on gender for all field staff (4 days)	Facilitated by women from inside to reflect on gender in livelihoods, gender and ecology	Development of facilitation skills, deepening practice of gender awareness programmes
Capacity building for women staff (3 days)	Special training for women staff in Prakruti through one-to-one and group discussions	Empowerment among women staff, gender awareness within teams, women recognizing gendering at the personal and organisational level, built capacity of women in Prakruti
	Assessment *Continuous Inputs*	
Monthly field visits to gauge changes	Observation and documentation	Record of changes in the community
	Exit	
Documentation		Document not shared with stakeholders, perceived as intrusive and done without consideration of the convenience of the community

APPENDIX 5.1

Concept of Gender

The concepts of gender used throughout the intervention process were:

- Gender is part biology and part social construct. It is enmeshed in the social relationships between man and woman. Gender is largely in the realm of attitudes; values and stereotypes that translates into objective realities such as roles, skills, opportunities, choices, and power relations.
- Gender is also about the 'masculine' and 'feminine' ways of perceiving and responding to life.
- Integrating gender is an equity issue. As it deals with inequalities between women and men and it involves power relations, equity issues cannot be covered without looking at gender. Therefore, even within the different disadvantaged groups, the issue of gender is a crosscutting theme.
- Gender is contextual. The heterogeneity in the social structure in our communities gives rise to multiple facets of gender. Gender intersects every caste, class, and community. Understanding gender issues has to be accompanied by a thorough understanding of the context of its occurrence. Therefore, gender cannot be generalised.
- As gender is contextual, there is no single way of addressing gender inequalities. Hence, this demands continuous innovation and creativity in evolving responses to the situation.
- Integrating gender involves not only bringing women and men on board but goes beyond numbers to more substantive or qualitative issues of changes in gender relations. Hence, integrating gender needs to be process-oriented with an action-reflection-learning cycle. In addition to what is being done, it is about how it is being done.

Given this, mainstreaming gender is a continuous enquiry towards change processes.

Appendix 5.2

Profile of a Gender Sensitive Organisation

1 less developed
5 well developed

Sl No	*Characteristics*	*1 2 3 4 5*
1.	Equal numbers of men and women across all levels and functions	
2.	Gender equality is a priority not only in the organisation's mission statement, general objectives and policies but also in its internal regulations (recruitment procedures, terms and conditions for workers, and so on)	
3.	Provides opportunities for women to work. They are not disadvantaged because of organisational norms	
4.	True participation of men and women–not politically correct only	
5.	Masculine and feminine qualities are given equal importance	
6.	Make resources available across gender, class and caste–within and outside	
7.	Work for women's empowerment and transformation of gender relations–not politically correct	
8.	Organic, process oriented working style is also encouraged	
9.	Interconnectedness between the different sectors/ units-holistic	
10.	Less hierarchical style of management that is open to change and oriented towards training, support, good feedback and stimulating colleagues.	
11.	Multiple leadership–not only designated leaders	
12.	Management-staff relations should be as non-vertical as possible: open, consultative and listening.	

(*Appendix 5.2 continued*)

(*Appendix 5.2 continued*)

Sl No	*Characteristics*	*1 2 3 4 5*
13.	Power is used to include not exclude	
14.	Team work is encouraged	
15.	Does not repeat traditional roles and responsibilities-provides opportunities to both women and men for taking on new roles.	
16.	Community- and client-entered	
17.	No rigid split between home and work.	
18.	Values different perspectives, diversity.	

Source: Mukhopadhyay et al. (2006)

Reference

Mukhopadhyay, M., G. Steehouwer, and F. Wong. 2006. *Politics of the Possible: Gender Mainstreaming and Organisational Change–Experiences from the Field.* POPLINE Document Number 312309. Amsterdam, The Netherlands: Royal Tropical Institute (KIT).

6

Case IV—Triveni

A Journey of Inclusion*

A Case Study Prepared under the C-POD Project for SRTT

The Context and the Institutions Involved
(Compiled by the C-POD Team)

Triveni is a government organisation responsible for drinking water supply and drainage in a state that lives virtually on the threshold of drought and faces severe depletion of groundwater levels.

The goal of the welfare state to ensure drinking water security in the decades following the 1960s saw the emergence of water praxis largely driven by the 'supply' approach. The compulsion to provide water at the earliest resulted in the creation of a large technocratic set-up under the aegis of the state. Central to the scheme was the role of professional water engineers who subscribed to a supply-driven approach, focusing primarily on the exploitation of ground water, to ensure supply of drinking water; initially by installing hand pumps, and subsequently through overhead tanks and pipelines. In the long run however, this approach gave rise to

---

* The intervention process was conducted during end-2003 to end-2006. An independent assessment was conducted in December 2005

'unintended and unforeseen' consequences. The approach, which presumed that 'water was waiting to be tapped and extracted through sound technology' encouraged unbridled water consumption and laid the foundation for future water crisis.

Another fallout of this approach was the inevitable distancing of the community from the problem and the urgency of sustainable solutions, displacing traditional practitioners and water management systems. Though totally unintended, the devaluation of traditional water management knowledge and skills played a major role in the erosion of community-based traditions of water use, conservation and protection from overuse, and the decline of community-generated and grounded initiatives to conserve local water sources. Consequently, any attempt to revive or reinvigorate the drinking water sector would therefore necessarily require the rediscovery of best practices from the old systems, and a need to integrate them with the knowledge gained from modern experiences.

The 1990s represented a period of critical re-examination of the supply-driven, technology-oriented, government-centred, and implementation-focused approaches. As Planning Commission (2001) noted in the Tenth Plan Approach Paper:

> Emphasis must be laid on the participation of stakeholders at all levels, from planning, design and location, to implementation and management. Presently, water supply projects are designed and executed by the implementing departments and passed on to end users... this calls for radical change in the management system. Rather than being supply-driven, the decision relating to installation of water supply schemes should be based on the level of local demand and capabilities to meet the responsibility for operation and maintenance.

A challenging scenario presented itself to all those involved with water in its varied dimensions at the start of the new millennium. Despite heavy rains, the first five years of the new millennium witnessed the cumulative impact of years of poor monsoon in the state and the unregulated mining of water and un-coordinated use for irrigation and industry, all aggravating the already precarious situation. This only highlighted the deleterious effect of the absence of a rational and integrated water policy framework.

The pressing water crisis created the need to come up with new solutions and called for a change in public policy, shifting the focus away from state- or government-driven mechanisms of water management to systems based on increased participation of the community, local bodies, and stakeholders. It was natural that the obvious starting point of the search for a solution lay with the agency entrusted with the responsibility of providing drinking water–Triveni. The changing nature of the water crisis forced a rethink on the best manner of managing water as a finite, precious, and precariously poised resource, as also an examination of the character and role of water providers and managers.

Institutional Transformation Group (ITG), the group that the consultant identified and invited to work with the system, had experience of working with several large government systems. Its commitment to this process came from an overall understanding of the pressures of globalisation operating on public systems and an interest to work on strengthening itself internally. The ITG describes itself as partners for facilitation or intervention. They are well known as rights activists and are sometimes at loggerheads with the very same administrative machinery. Two resource persons from ITG worked together initially till a few resource persons were developed within the system itself. Subsequently, only one person from ITG remained involved.

The process began towards the end of 2003 and the series of workshops were concluded by the end of 2006.

An independent assessment, of the impact was taken up in December 2005 and the report was completed in March 2006. An informal interview with the consultant and the internal leader of the change programme in January 2006 was helpful in capturing the challenges they faced in the process.

The OD Process and Event Structure

(Based on the Formal Documentation)

This report is a record of the experience of Triveni, which initiated a process of critically reviewing its practices and values, its work culture and performance, its vision and achievements. Arising from this churning began the process of organisational transformation. In a sense this report will never be complete as it is the saga of a history which is continually being shaped, and consequently, constantly undergoing changes. But to the extent that the report is a testimony of experiences it presents an opportunity to share with others the possibilities, joys, and difficulties of

Figure 6.1 Organisational Structure of Triveni

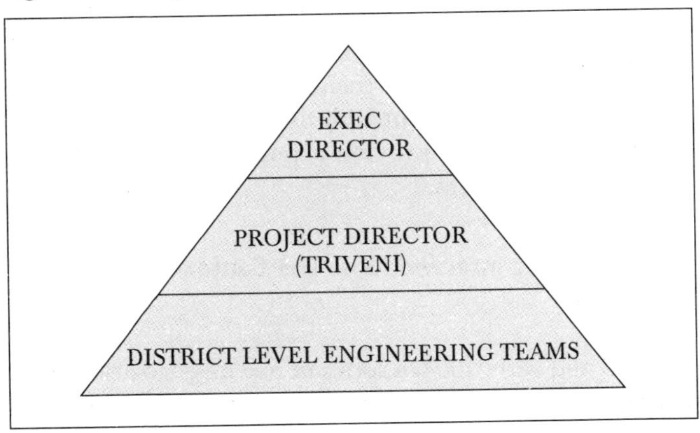

Figure 6.2 The Intervention Cycle for Triveni

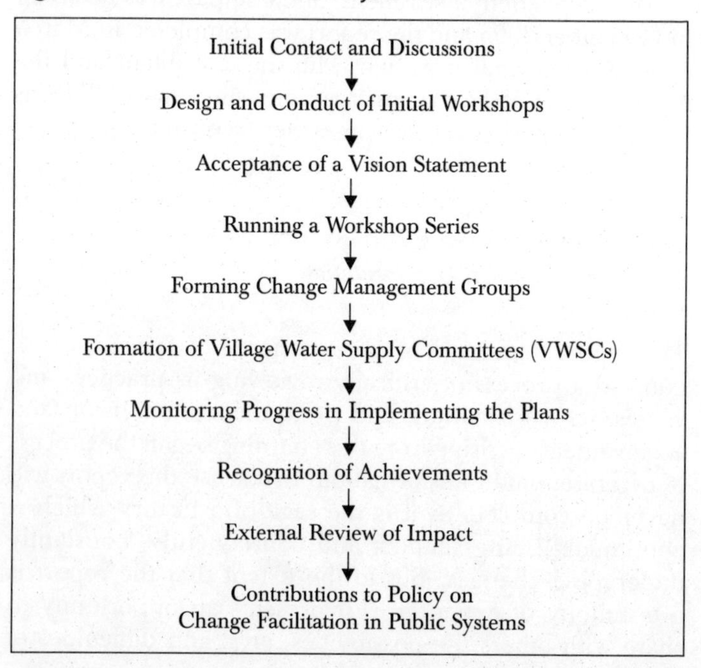

initiating a change process to improve the delivery systems of critical services like water. The intention of documenting the experiences is also to share with and invite those concerned to become 'co-travellers' with the participants of the change experiment with the hope that lessons from this experiment will provide a model for an alternative governance paradigm.

Initial Training Interventions: The Context of the 2003 Exercises

In 2003 and early 2004, a series of meetings, focused group discussions and three-day workshops were held covering all engineers attached to the rural water supply sector. Thus, while there was widespread dissemination about the new paradigm and changed expectations, the extent of assimilation was not clear. The response of the engineers was one of tacit acceptance of the new community orientation thrust as that was now the stated policy of the government. Beyond that, there was little or no feedback or engagement, reflecting true internalisation.

What had to be urgently addressed was the issue of attitudinal changes amongst engineers who were now being asked to play new roles of becoming 'social engineers' which required them to perform engineering functions within a social matrix. In such a scenario they were required not only to deal with scientific facts and technology issues but also to be sensitive to social dynamics.

The Churning Process: Some Glimpses

The difficulty that arose was that there was no forum or established process within the organisation's functioning which could facilitate a process of open and critical exploration. Hierarchy-bound and status-conscious practices also inhibited open exchange amongst even those few who perceived the nature of challenge and crisis before them. It was in such a context that the present transformation intervention process was initiated and a pair of external resource persons invited to help plan, implement and partner major change exercises throughout the organisation.

The Koodam

The transformation process began with an invitation to the members of the board participating in the process to create a *Koodam* in which they could interact with each other as equals, engage in the common purpose of learning from as well as with one another without the distinction of rank, position or privilege. The *Koodam* is actually a traditional concept and practice in the society with parallels like the *Choupal* and others.

Koodam refers to a geographical space in a village that is held sacred and where all participants–adult members of the society meet as equals to discuss issues and arrive at some kind of consensus. Within the *Koodam*, the norms for relating as members are based on the acceptance that all are equal irrespective of differences in status, wealth and learning. *Koodam* is an honoured sacred space that all participants value and respect.

The series of change management workshops culminated with a major breakthrough in the fourth workshop. The churning process resulted in evolving a new paradigm of operation by the engineers themselves. This came to be known as the 'Triveni Declaration'.

Building a Shared Vision

Initially, there was resistance and opposition to the declaration among the officials/organisation. Some saw in it a criticism of past policies; others saw it as striking at the very core of the operations of the organisation and felt that the declaration was not saying anything new. Yet others saw it as articulating something that many felt but had not yet put together as a perspective for action. In order to evolve a consensus, discussions were initiated at formal and informal levels throughout the organisation on the declaration. Naturally, issues of water crisis, sustainability, the role of Triveni and the need to initiate change were debated.

Despite the contested nature of the declaration, slowly a consensus evolved that it was not only acceptable, but also required to be pushed through within the organisation with the involvement of other stakeholders. The process of widening the consensus was strengthened when the district collectors, various policy makers, and other opinion makers were brought on board. They then endorsed the declaration, thus ensuring its complete acceptance prior to implementation.

What is noteworthy is that the declaration was also shared with a cross section of civil society. The build-up of support ensured that the declaration did not remain just a rhetorical statement but an article of faith, guiding future interventions across the state.

The adoption of the declaration and the subsequent endorsement by the secretary, municipal administration, water supply department, managing director of Triveni and other senior officials set the stage for the next phase of the transformation exercise in the organisation.

Box 6.1 The Shared Vision

Secure water for all, forever...

- Conservation of nature as a guarantee for the future of water
- Vibrant, revived and recharged water bodies
- Assured, equitable and sustainable water for all
- A successful community-managed water supply system through active participation of women and the poor
- Safe disposal of solid and liquid waste for a clean and healthy environment
- Cost-effective technology options to ensure local maintenance and sustainability
- Financial management
- Formation of common water regulatory authority for the judicious use of water for all sectors

The draft vision was shared throughout the organisation at the district- and field-levels and was endorsed on World Water Day 2005 by the organisation and policy makers. It was also shared with the community in 145 project village panchayats.

Formation of the Change Management Group (CMG)

The increasing acceptance and implementation of the declaration pushed the change process to the next phase, emphasising the need for formation of a core group at the state level, which would then spearhead all change activities. Whether members decided to undertake change projects aimed at increasing employee morale or on evolving a comprehensive database or conducting similar training interventions, it soon became apparent that all future change or transformation efforts would need to be coordinated and planned. This led to the formation of a change management group (CMG) at the state level.

Building on the norms introduced through the workshops and the spirit of the declaration, CMG members were those who volunteered to be part of the exercise. Their work as CMG participants would be over and beyond their regular work and they would not get any special concessions or rewards for being CMG members. Care was taken to ensure that the CMG had representatives from different age groups, covering all the regions of the state, and covering a cross-section of people. The newly-formed CMG evolved its own mandate for functioning:

- To work further on the outcome and strategise for change.
- To develop skills in managing change through pilot projects.
- To be an in-house group for dialogue with the rest of the system.
- To facilitate empowering, capacity-building and creating a core team to envision and lead the change process.
- To cover all employees as associates.

After detailed deliberations and introspection at both formal and informal levels, the CMG members decided to identify and imbibe certain values by which they would like to be identified. The group committed itself to upholding these values in all their transactions–be it as individuals or as an organisation.

Change Projects

The CMG initiated projects to demonstrate to itself and to the rest of the organisation its commitment to the change process, as well as to showcase the potential uncovered by the process. The CMG took up change projects around three broad areas of activities:

- People-oriented–focusing on the impact on people, both internally as well as externally.

Box 6.2 Projects Identified by CMG

People-oriented

- Community water supply and sanitation micro plan
- Institution building–village user committee formation in Gram Sabha
- Revival of traditional water bodies
- Ground water demand management
- Involvement of school children–'Our Water'

Task-oriented

- Spot settlement of audit observations
- Formation of e-groups and interaction among members

Process-oriented

- *Koodam* internalisation–monthly meetings
- Creation of new *koodams*–practicing at district offices
- Newsletter–encrypting the activities and sharing experiences
- Launching and stabilising district-level CMG

- Task-oriented–focusing on issues related to work and the formal areas of organisational functioning.
- Process-oriented–encompassing issues of communication systems, decision-making processes within the organisation, leadership within the organisation, and other related issues.

Developing the Intervention Design

The building blocks of the transformation process were based on the following understanding of the context that the facilitators developed.

Shifts in Mind Sets

The Triveni board enjoyed an exclusive mandate for providing water supply and the water board executives functioned as exclusive specialists answerable only as providers. The challenges of the water crisis however dramatically altered their situation and context. Detailed internal deliberations led to the identification of the need for a community-based approach to ensure sustainable water systems. Thus from being sole decision makers, the water managers now had to function as a body whose future was intrinsically linked with community choice. The exploration naturally had to cover the issues of social, cultural and economic relations and forces. Strategically, this process required a conscious intervention focus on:

- Attitudinal changes amongst individuals comprising the manner in which individuals perceive their own roles and functions and the nature of relationship between themselves, the water board, and the community at large.

- Attitudinal changes within the organisation comprising the manner in which the organisation relates to the ordinary citizen who is now being addressed as a 'consumer' of the services offered by the board, with the aim of reaching the un-reached.
- Attitudinal changes among the key stakeholders comprise the larger change effort to include a concurrent change in the way other stakeholders and the community at large perceive the relevance and importance of the board and the services it offers. This is premised on the fact that where people see possibilities of a meaningful and purposive interaction with the service provider they will naturally engage in a sustained relationship for mutual benefit, leading to sustainable and equitable services.

The Thrust of Institutional Change

The Triveni board, a repository of the accumulated wisdom, knowledge, and experiences of hundreds of highly qualified engineers is a vast treasure house of information about the water sector in the state. It is thus strategic to utilise the technocratic and managerial expertise of the board as the starting point to transform the organisation into a more people-focused, community-responsive, and publicly accountable organisation. The dynamics of this change process therefore covered the following dimensions:

- Ensuring 'convergent community action' by bringing together state service providers and officials with an active, involved and better informed community.
- Establishing a meaningful interface between community and service delivery systems.
- Ensuring convergence and coherence in policy formulation, planning and implementation.

- Strengthening service delivery systems by focusing on improving efficiency and effectiveness of individuals and systems and self-sustaining change efforts.
- Capacity-building of different stakeholders, including government officials, women and local communities, local bodies, and NGO representatives and elected representatives.

Some Basic Assumptions

The training effort was premised on the following important assumptions:

- Individuals should be willing and committed to exploring the need for change in themselves and the department.
- Senior officials in the department should openly exhibit their own willingness and readiness to work for bringing about change and be ready to lead by personal example.
- Sustaining individual-level changes by supportive responses of institution. Individual-level changes will be sustained and successful only when the system also demonstrates its readiness to stand by individuals during the process of bringing about a more efficient, responsive, and human concern-based system.
- Just as individual behaviour reflects one's own sense of values, attitudes, norms, vision, culture and worldviews, systems too reflect similar characteristics.
- Change projects can succeed only when they address the imperatives of change at both the individual and system levels in the entirety of issues discussed.

These assumptions were made explicit to the senior management and the clarity developed around these assumptions proved important for the next stage.

The Training Design: Three Core Thrust Areas

There were essentially three thrust areas covered in the training design.

Breaking Barriers—Building Bridges

Addressing issues related to the 'person' and the 'personal', exploring the ways in which people relate to one another and creating a climate of camaraderie based on shared experiences and group learning.

Confronting Challenges—Creating Convergences

Exploring issues of collective living and survival as members with differing interests. Examining issues of water management with consideration for each other's priorities and the corresponding conflicts.

Synergising Strengths—Strategising Success

Examining the strengths of different stakeholders which are critical to the success of any venture like this, to bring about synergy in the use of energies and resources, and evolving strategies to ensure success of such schemes in a practical manner in the actual field context.

The Basic Construct

The difficulties of working in a hierarchical government system made it necessary to address some critical issues at the very beginning of the process.

- To break the hierarchical approach of relating and encourage free interaction.

- To ensure people do not take recourse to strategic 'silence' in the presence of seniors.
- To prevent people from saying 'yes' when they actually mean 'no'.
- To instil a sense of individual and collective ownership of the process of change.

This was done through the use of *Koodam* as a safe occasion to try and break out of this mould. The facilitators had to demonstrate their commitment to these new norms as the initial stage for transformation. Initially only a few would take the risk but gradually others would follow. Sometimes there remained a few who were still not convinced even at the end of the workshop. The facilitators had to learn to accept all these responses with equanimity.

Integrating Learning through Field Visits

Intrinsic to the learning process was to integrate the critical and open reflection process initiated in workshops with actual field conditions. Based on the recommendations of participants of the preliminary workshops, field visits were incorporated into the training design so that members involved in the reflection exercise were made to engage with field conditions and include the perspectives of the people they were meant to serve. This part of the training matrix enabled a reality check and ensured that the reflective exercise was anchored in actual village conditions.

The design of the intervention stabilised and the main events were a series of workshops with 30 to 35 participants. Over a period of four to five days the participating members explored numerous issues covering their work. The workshops concluded with the participants identifying specific actions at the three levels. These plans were kept track of and the achievements acknowledged and recognised formally.

The Journey Continues–Next Steps

The encouraging response to the various change projects initiated by the CMG and other members of Triveni and the gradually evolving external support for the efforts of the CMG led it to prepare for the second year of the larger transformation exercise–to institutionalise change management within the practice and praxis of the organisation and to begin the process of exploring the issues impacting working relationships, work culture and performance within the organisation.

Reflections of the Facilitators

(Based on Interviews between Triveni Project Director and the ITG Team for CPOD)

Introduction

The role of the state as a provider of basic services is being reinvented with emphasis on its special responsibility to safeguard the interests of the marginalised or vulnerable segments of the community in today's globalised scenario. It is in this context that the change efforts in Triveni become a significant example to learn from. The case typifies the challenges of attempting a large system change. In this section, the nature of the relationship between the change facilitators and department is discussed.

Entry Stage

The context for the OD effort was a sharp water crisis and the recognition that the problems within the system had to be addressed and not externalised (in terms of monsoon failure, public apathy, and so on). A process-based OD effort was sought when conceptual inputs seemed to have limited impact on the technical cadres. The conceptual analysis and the resultant prescription for change were in fact resented both within the department and by the facilitators. Thus the facilitators and the management were opposed to the recovery of user charges without recognising the socio-economic differences among the user communities.

The Background

The resource persons chosen for the intervention process had a background as rights activists and are in legal practice. They were formally trained in management being alumni of TISS. They had an interest in safeguarding public service because they believed that this was the only way to safeguard the interests of the less powerful segments of society. They have had numerous experiences of working with large systems and the approach they adopted for this project had been developed gradually over the years. Their work was supported by a bilateral agency.

Introducing OD to the Department

Not being readily accepted by the technical cadres, establishing their credibility was a challenge that the facilitators faced at the entry stage. The language of OD seemed to pose problems both for the resource persons and the user system. Thus terms like 'consultant', 'client' and 'diagnoses' were carefully avoided. The resource persons consistently introduced themselves as rights activists who were involved in this partnership to facilitate change. Some of the terms used to describe the interest of the facilitator were their interest in water justice; their pro-public sector bias; and their rights rather than management perspective.

In preferring this identity they were demonstrating their commitment to the outcome of their effort. Another important aspect was the issue of consultancy fee–the facilitators were paid a 'local' fee for their work throughout the process and were clearly not there as a 'corollary' to a large grant or loan. This too was well known within the department. This came out as a major proof of the good intentions of ITG.

Negotiation with Project Management

The word 'contract' was again 'unacceptable' within the context of the department and therefore avoided. However there was good clarity and understanding between the facilitators and the project management before they embarked on the change facilitation process.

They negotiated with the project director for continued support for the process at the very outset clarifying that results could not be guaranteed, especially if the effort was to be abandoned halfway. The consistent support for the process from the project director thus became a crucial factor for success. The recurring differences between the project director and the executive director (the overall boss) did not however stop the process in any way but perhaps accounts for the non-adoption of the process in other similar systems despite the demonstrated success. This project also rebuts the theme of restructuring public services through liberalisation of market forces and thus runs counter to popular prescriptions on the topic.

Partnership for Interventions

The term for the external resource persons that was mutually acceptable in this context was the word 'partnership'. The partnership was for facilitation and intervention.

The notion of partnership was further developed through identifying a core group of technocrats within the system with the requisite skill and conviction about the agenda for change. These officials in turn became the co-facilitators who would conduct the workshops along with the external facilitators. This became functional because the external facilitators would keep clear of any claims to technical expertise and rely instead, on the in-house collaborators for such inputs when the need arose. The district-level change management groups evolved from the workshop process took charge of further action and the implementation of changes in the field. Thus the onus for action clearly stayed within the system at all levels.

Thresholds of Resistance

The programmes brought to the surface a lot of resistance from within the organisation and these layers had to be gradually peeled away before any real change could be attempted. The levels and intensity of resistance indicated that the exercise would be difficult. Some of the methods which were repeatedly used to address such resistance included field visits, open discussions, examination of all doubts especially those pertaining to the usefulness of this process, and so on. It needed a special effort to hold to the norms of interaction so that trust was developed gradually. Some typical issues that came up were:

- Theoretical rather than practical knowledge of the facilitators.
- Presumed vested interests of the facilitators.
- External problems such as politics, weather, and so on.
- Problems with user communities.
- Technical issues.

These were patiently dealt with in each workshop and all the engineers were gradually covered. Creating a safe forum for the participants to freely share their doubts and reservations was a task faced by the facilitators. Use of local idioms, setting up of 'whispering box' (a closed box with a slit for people to drop their suggestions and concerns, anonymously or otherwise), insisting on creation of some ground rules within the workshop, maintaining congruence between what was said and what was done were very important. As they crossed this threshold of mistrust and fear, participants overcame their reluctance and accepted their shortcomings. This was the point at which they were ready to look at how they contributed to the crisis and how they can change. The facilitators looked for 'hooks' in the scenarios built by the groups–these were the points that could be used to build change agendas. A lot of similes, allegories and exercises were developed and used.

Processes to Consolidate the Change

As the groups experienced their own transition in the course of a workshop the facilitators too gradually shifted their stance. This levelling was an indicator of having dealt with the resistance within the group. As each workshop identified an agenda for action, the internal change management groups consolidated these plans and kept track of the actual action on the ground. When the plans were acted upon appreciation letters went out from the project director. Similarly, appreciation from the community was also shared. Work and performance standards were developed by the engineers themselves and these were adopted to assess the performance.

Role of the Project Director

The project director remained a firm internal anchor for the whole process. He supported the project by locating resource persons, developing their brief and standing by his commitments to them. He also supported the process of these workshops shielding it from external threats, especially at the initial stages and coordinating the details of implementation even though he continued to face tough questions from his superiors.

The concrete action-steps became most important in strengthening the change. The doubts in the minds of the engineers about the continuance of such support after the PD was transferred were openly discussed, but the action plans had developed in such a robust way that they had become self-sustaining, gathering a force of their own and could still be implemented. It is interesting to note that the PD has been able to stay on despite conflicts within the board and with external power centres, and is now planning for another such intervention within the sector.

Internalising Change—An Assessment

(Compiled from the Detailed Report of An Independent Reviewer–March 2006)

The capacity-building intervention was from the beginning conceptualised in field reality. In a sense, the project villages were the experimental workspaces to implement many of the new concepts learnt through the exploratory process of group learning in the workshop.

There was a symbiotic relationship between the workshop and the project villages which were used as laboratories to test the newfound insights of democratic water management and exorcise their minds of the apprehensions about giving a voice and choice to the community. The state-wide projects involved about 80 rural water supply subdivisions of the Triveni board. The focus of the project was to take up a holistic approach to water supply by involving the community in formulation, implementation and subsequent management of the water supply system, including the revival of traditional practices. The fruits of this new way of thinking and working started manifesting early, highlighting the potential of such change processes in improving the delivery systems of vital services. Some of the important outcomes have been discussed in the following paragraphs.

Community Contribution

As a measure of the involvement of the community and its sense of ownership, the project envisaged 10 per cent of the capital cost as community contribution in cash or labour. Over a one-year period the community had contributed Rs 13.5 million in cash apart from various *shramdaans*, with nearly 35,000 households contributing to implementing the water supply or recharge schemes in 145 village panchayats.

Cost Reduction

One of the most significant impacts which portray the inherent potential of this process of personal and institutional change is the reduction in the capital cost per household by 40 per cent in the project villages. It has been found that the average cost per household in the regular schemes was about Rs 4,436 (on habitation basis), whereas in the pilot batch, the average cost was only Rs 1,555 (on village basis). In real terms this means the possibility of an additional coverage of four lakh households every year within the same budget.

Cost-effective Solutions

Nearly 50 per cent of the schemes (106 out of 210) are low capital intensive, focusing mostly on rehabilitation of the earlier investments. This reflects a different way of decision-making, based on community ownership, choice and willingness to manage the operating costs.

Better Targeting

Under the project, about 65 per cent of the schemes were targeted at villages with more than 50 per cent below poverty line (BPL) population. This is in sharp contrast to the generally low targeting of such groups under regular schemes.

Savings

In line with the declaration, many of the districts have taken up vigorous scrutiny of all investment proposals in the search of sustainable and cost-effective solutions. The savings over the annual budget has been as high as Rs 10.70 million and Rs 16.60 million in two districts (varying between eight to 33 per cent of the budget). In fact, in one of the districts the team had utilised the savings to take up a unique community participatory source rehabilitation programme in 220 habitations by involving the community in decision making and financing the projects.

Planning

In all the 145 village panchayats, detailed village water supply master plans were prepared by the community with the assistance of the engineers and approved in the Gram Sabha. The master plans had sub-plans on ground water recharge, water quality, and environmental issues including subsequent management and financing issues. Only those schemes which figured in the approved master plans were taken up for implementation.

Institution Building

It was felt necessary to provide a formal forum for the community to spearhead its water and sanitation interventions. For this purpose village water and sanitation committees (VWSCs) were proposed in all the project villages. In all 157 VWSCs were formed in the project villages by the community with the approval of the Gram Sabha. The unique feature of the VWSC was that there was a positive bias towards the disadvantaged. The women's self-help group leader was the treasurer of the VWSC, and 1/4th memberships were earmarked for women. The community was also convinced and they agreed to provide adequate representation to the SC and ST population of the village. The Triveni board engineers had many structured and informal interactions with the VWSCs and focus groups for capacity-building and to provide assistance in tackling water and sanitation issues of the village, including mobilising the community towards self-management.

Conservation and Recharge

The finiteness of water availability was a constant message of the project. The community was encouraged to take up ground water recharge activities including revival of traditional water bodies as a first step to revisit historical practices of community living and sharing of scarce resources. Water balance studies informing the status of water availability at the micro level for the village was carried out in all the 145 village panchayats and shared with the community.

The community also participated in the physical implementation of 45 ground water recharge schemes. In all, the project villages special Gram Sabhas were convened on 2 October and 26 January during the project period (2004–2006) to take up cleaning and revival of traditional water bodies.

Lessons for Change Managers

The experiences in the 'democratisation of the water management project' has thrown up a lot of lessons for the policy makers, the organisation, as well as for the individuals involved in the project. Many of the lessons are diffused at the moment, as the process is still unfolding. But the experiences would surely live on in the organisation as stories retold in keeping with the strong oral traditions of India. We have sought to capture the experiences of change not merely to record the history, but also as a means to help others learn from the experiences.

The CMG, an offshoot of this change process, has attempted to bring these field-level change processes into the formal organisational memory by documenting the various experiences and outcomes of the process. It may be important to stress at this point that these are just glimpses of the plethora of issues that have been thrown up by this churning at the field level.

Towards Total Community Water Management

To breathe life and to give concrete shape to the vision, the CMG has taken up community-based projects in 100 villages across the state. As a first step to achieving the dream it has undertaken to implement a time-bound project to test some of the essential lessons of the various change efforts initiated by them. Out of this process emerged the project titled, 'Total Community Water Management'.

Though very encouraging as mentioned at the beginning, this is an ongoing process and requires the continuous support and involvement, of not only the board and local administration, but also the central and state governments and the international financial institutions that fund these schemes and projects. And that is the greatest challenge–convincing these higher authorities, policy-makers, and institutions, about the new arrangement. A change in their mindset has to be brought about.

OD Tools and Techniques

(Based on the Formal Documentation)

Understanding the Water Crisis: Am I Part of the Problem?

An important issue that needed to be addressed was for the participants to consider the question as to (*i*) whether there was a water problem at all, and (*ii*) if there was indeed a problem, where did they see themselves vis-à-vis the problem?

This exercise was the most challenging and difficult of exercises but nevertheless, a crucial stage to be crossed. Different methods were adopted depending on the group.

A case study followed by a game called the 'Survival Exercise' was also played which sought to address the issue of making difficult choices without excluding others. An important learning point was the realisation that only when a problem is understood properly will appropriate or sound solutions be found. The exercise was then contrasted with the specifics of the water management situation in rural areas of the state.

Table 6.1 Analysis of Tools and Techniques—Triveni
(Based on the Formal Documentation)

Activity	*Methodology*	*Impact/Outcomes*
	Entry	
Initial contact and discussions	Series of meetings, focus group discussions and 3-day workshops in which case studies and survival exercises to understand the water crisis were used	Implicit acceptance of the new shift in orientation, no feedback regarding true internalisation, to address the issue of attitudinal change, to move towards new role of social engineer, lack of forum to facilitate exploration
	Diagnosis and Design of Interventions	
Design and conduct of initial workshops	Interaction of board members with engineers on an equal basis using Koodam, Johari Windows adapted, Force Field Analysis, and Field visits	New paradigm of operation called Triveni Declaration
	Intervention	
Acceptance of a vision statement	Formal and informal discussions about the Declaration throughout the organisation	Consensus that the statement not only needed to be accepted but also pushed throughout the organisation, District Collectors' and policy makers' endorsement of the Vision, Sharing of the statement with cross section of the civil society; stage set for next phase

	Running Workshop Series	
Forming change management groups	Voluntary body of representatives covering all age groups and regions of the state	Evolved its own mandate and values for functioning, initiated projects to show commitment towards change, projects focused on impact on people within and without the organisation, issues related to work, processes such as communication, decision making, and so on
Formation of VWSCs	Formed in the project villages with the approval of Gram Sabha, 1/4th membership for women and adequate representation of SCs and STs	Mobilizing community towards self-management, tackling of water and sanitation issues
	Assessing Impact	
Monitoring progress in implementing the plan, recognition of achievements, external review of impact.		
	Exit	
Contributions to policy on change facilitation in public systems, Emergence of 'Total Community Water Management'.		

While there was initially strong resistance, both at the conscious and unconscious levels, to critically examine their own role in the water crisis, as the workshop progressed members were more willing to accept that they had a role, both in being part of the problem, as also in being part of the solution.

The *Koodam*

In a dramatic manner, the concept of *Koodam* helped establish a new sense of relating, belongingness, and purpose for the officials who had been invited to be part of the exercise to bring about changes within the organisation. The officials ranged from chief engineers to assistant engineers.

While participants responded at different levels at the end of each workshop, due to the *Koodam* most participants were considerably open and non-defensive while looking at the various issues, including the need to change themselves and the way they functioned.

The norms for the interactions in the *Koodam* were introduced and all participants were gradually included in the group. The facilitators could build authenticity by truthfully acknowledging all the externalities and the risks that came with greater openness. The issues that came up such as political factors, different levels of support and commitment among the senior officials in the board were not trivialised or evaded. The group was gently nudged to go beyond these fears and doubts by invoking their humaneness and overall social responsibility.

The Adapted Johari Window

The Johari Window was adapted to the workshop's needs to create awareness of the prevalence of blind spots at both individual and institutional levels, and to provoke exploration about the effect of such blind spots. There was a marked difference between the views before and after the discussions following the field visits. The visits challenged the participants to think 'out of the box' and compelled them to reflect on issues which they had either never considered to be their responsibility or something in which they alone had a role. At the end of the exercise many participants had changed the understanding of their role as not only involving the exercising of responsibility in the specific areas of their expertise and competencies, but also in becoming proactive change agents, catalysing other departments to arrive at a more holistic, integrated, and comprehensive sustainable solution to the water crisis confronting the state. The most interesting shift was seeing the issue from the prism of a purely technical framework to comprehending the challenge from a larger, socially and professionally inclusive perspective.

Force Field Analysis—Creating Strategic Action Plans

A major stage in the workshop revolved around the Force Field Activity exercise. Participants were introduced to the fact that any change process has to contend with supportive or resisting (obstructive) forces, which emanate from both internal and external sources. Members were then guided to identify these forces separately in the specific context of rural water supply. The next exercise was to categorise these forces into five sub-categories in both supportive and resisting forces.

The usefulness of the Force Field Analysis was not that it was teaching anything new to those who had been dealing with interest groups for many years. The method helped identify forces in a conscious and deliberate manner and then studied what role each 'force' played in supporting or obstructing the process of change. The exercise enabled participants to identify measures to enhance supportive forces and to tackle resistive or obstructive ones. The combined effect was to help evolve strategic action plans for the implementation of change projects in select villages.

Village Visit: Learning from Critiquing Existing Schemes

During the workshops the participants were divided into teams, which then visited three villages. During the debriefing discussions critical questions were raised about the various projects found in the villages and whether they stood to scrutiny based on the varieties of issues covered during the workshop especially from the viewpoint of stakeholders.

The board's own projects in the village were analysed in terms of its environmental-economic need/impact, and the importance of studying the viability of the scheme in terms of sustainability and cost of O&M. The field reality, through the glasses of hindsight, in the context of the present water scarcity, really shook up the participants.

Reference

Planning Commission. 2001. *Approach Paper to the Tenth Five Year Plan (2002–2007)*. New Delhi: Govt of India.

7

Case V—Panchim

A Story of Renewal

*A Case Study Prepared under the C-POD Project Supported by SRTT**

The Context and the Institutions Involved

(Compiled by the C-POD Team)

An important banking development after nationalisation was the emergence of the social banking concept. In the 1970s, the banking policy was reoriented to ensure that the benefits of development percolate sufficiently to the needy. Thus, regional rural banks (RRBs) like Panchim emerged to supplement the weak co-operative system and the commercial banking operations in rural areas. Panchim was promoted jointly by a major national financial institution (NFI), and the State and Central Governments. It functions in a chronic poverty zone as the key linking mechanism between the rural/regional and the urban/national financial markets. A crucial member in the financial sector, it bears the load of the flows between these two layers. Oriented to social banking, profitability was never its prime objective, though in the long run it was expected to become viable.

---

* The intervention process was conducted during July to December 2003. The review was conducted in September 2006.

The post-liberalisation reforms in the financial sector had a deep impact on rural finance institutions like these RRBs. They faced unrelenting pressure to adapt and evolve, and to provide better quality services to their customers. The concept of purely 'social-banking' had become irrelevant, and at the same time competition from other commercial establishments had intensified. They realised that major changes were needed to develop and deliver services in a cost-effective way to suit customer needs and yet remain viable. The discipline of asset classification and provisioning norms based on income recognition forced them to revisit their purpose and agenda. Many rural banks, particularly those operating in prosperous agricultural belts, quickly adapted to the changes and widened the scope of their activities to reap the benefits of liberalisation.

Such flexibility was more difficult for banks like Panchim, operating in extremely challenging and chronic poverty zones. Attempts to replicate the approach of the more favourably located RRBs did not prove successful; they had to find a route to sustainability through lending to the very poor in their area of operation. The customers also seemed unprepared to take advantage of any dramatic improvement in the volume, range and quality of banking service available. Their concern was to first resolve their basic food security and subsistence needs. The real banking need of such a rural customer-base had yet to be sharply defined.

The need for OD process in the Panchim RRB arose in this context. The sponsor of the change process was a large international NGO, Concern, which facilitated the development of a women's thrift and self-help movement through a string of local partner NGOs. The project soon recognised the need to work with the frontline service providers in the local rural banking system. They initiated the project and took it up with the NFI, the sponsor of Panchim.

They identified an OD consultant group–Reflect–which would prove to be credible to the banking system, and work with commitment to the agenda of financial inclusion in backward regions. They also located a local collaborator, Zeal, who would work within the overall design developed by Reflect in the local language.

The reflect team had a good understanding of banking as two of their senior consultants had over twenty years of experience in the financial sector at various levels. In addition, the lead consultant had professional training in process-based consultancy. The principal consultant of the local consultancy organisation Zeal had a decade of experience in development-related consultancy after his education in a leading business school. The main theme that ran through their work was of renewal.

The process was initiated in July 2003 and the various interventions were spread over six months up to December 2003. A review and exit was completed in May 2004. The large system implications of this project were also identified and presented in major national microfinance conferences and fed into the review of the rural financial system that was underway at that time.

A reviewer visited the organisation and interviewed change agents in September 2006, nearly three years after the first round of interventions.

The OD Process and Event Structure

(Based on the Formal Documentation)

The project started with a two-day preliminary meeting at the Central Office of the NFI. The meeting helped allay the anxiety of the chairman of Panchim and the detailed

Figure 7.1 Stakeholders in the Panchim OD Process

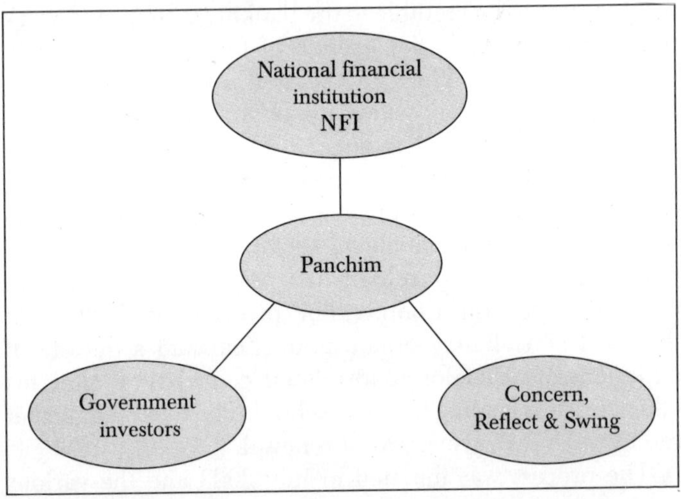

planning and scheduling of activities was concluded. The stages were defined as a cycle through the following steps: Discovery, diagnosis, design of strategy, recharging, performance and assessment. The major events in the OD process are described below.

Initial Surveys

A climate survey for the staff and a customer survey on service quality covering several locations were conducted with a resource person team drawn from Reflect and Concern. The consultant team interacted with the board of Panchim, presenting the OD plan and seeking their views. Interactions with union and officer association leaders were also very important steps. These interactions across different stakeholders helped in building a shared understanding about

Figure 7.2 The Intervention Cycle for Panchim

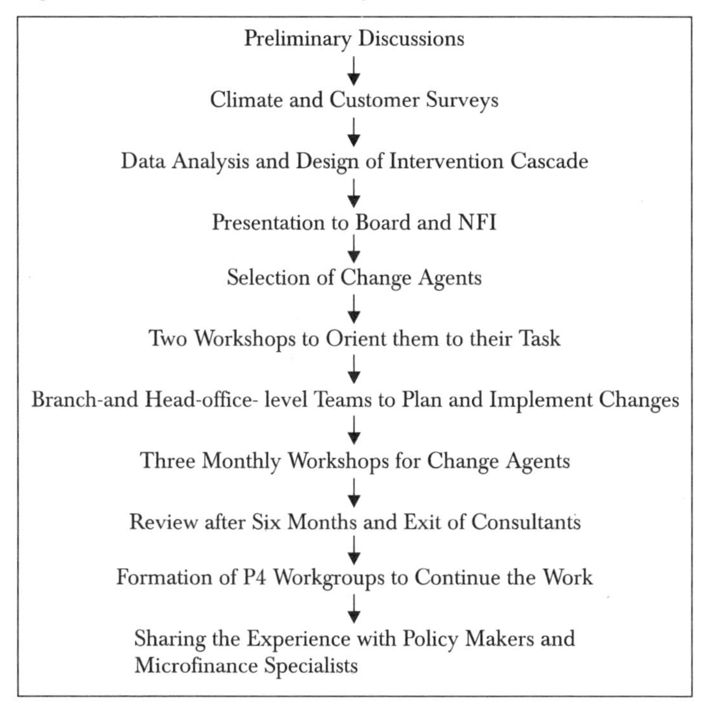

the scope of the OD process and gaining their support. Above all, it was useful to dispel rumours and misgivings by openly discussing them.

Change Agent Selection and Orientation

A cascade model to carry the message of change into the organisation and involve all layers of staff was designed by the Reflect team. Panchim identified change agents from across the hierarchy and their network of branches. Two senior

Figure 7.3 Organisational Structure of Panchim

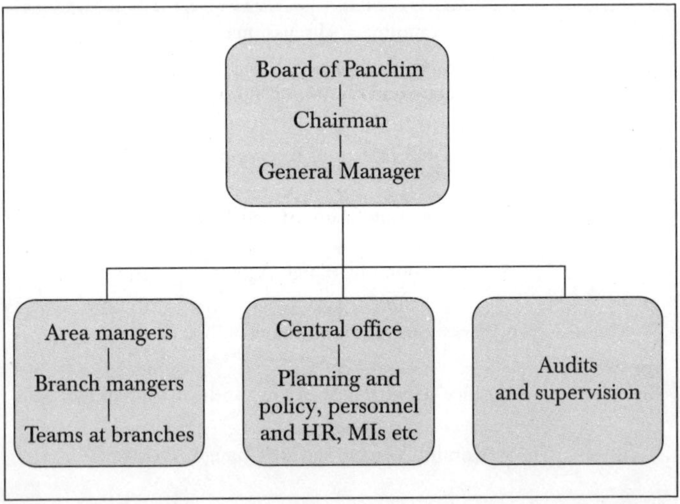

Board of Panchim
Chairman
General Manager

Area mangers
Branch mangers
Teams at branches

Central office
Planning and policy, personnel and HR, MIs etc

Audits and supervision

consultants from Reflect facilitated these workshops to orient the selected staff members to their task as change facilitators. The presence of senior representatives from NFI and Concern helped build credibility for the process. The workshops offered the space for the change agents to express their concerns and gradually buy into the change process. They were presented with the data collected and processed from the two surveys. The workshop concluded with detailed plans for branch-level discovery, diagnosis and action plans.

Workshops on Critical Themes

As the work in the branches progressed three more workshops were identified on critical themes in the diagnosis stage:

- Shared vision and customer orientation
- Credit management and recoveries
- Business development and profitability analysis.

These workshops were jointly facilitated by the consultants from Zeal and Reflect. The presence of the consultant from Zeal made the participants comfortable. They could express their views freely in the local language and they began to see him as 'one of their own'.

Review and Assessment Workshop

The impact of the change process was assessed and the ways of continuing the initiated work identified.

Detailed Description of the Steps

A mixture of standard and context-specific tools was used for this intervention. This had come from experience where the tools and techniques seem to approximate the settings like Panchim. Some were built based on the energy levels of the participants at the workshop.

Diagnostic Phase—Elements of the Diagnostic Survey

The diagnosis involved study of the following aspects, both at the district and branch levels.

- Operating environment survey.
- Market outreach analysis.
- Client feedback.
- Portfolio analysis.
- Assessment of training needs.
- Review of secondary sources.

The tools used for the purpose were:

- Customer surveys at branches.
- Focus group discussions with key constituents.
- Organisational climate survey.
- Focus group discussion with key stakeholders.
- Portfolio analysis.
- Skills inventory and analysis of training needs.

Customer Feedback

The customer surveys at branches were based on the 'expectations' approach to service quality covering six dimensions–tangibles, reliability, fulfilment of social concerns, responsiveness, empathy and assurance. These results were cross-checked with measures of service quality by using the 'specifications' approach already available within the system, and the findings from the Focus Group Discussions (FGDs) by the OD team.

The questionnaire was made available to all the branches. The branch managers talked to five 'important' customers and five 'random' customers. Important customers were those who contributed significant levels of business to the branch. Random customers could have any level of business. Each staff member talked to five customers, at least three of whom were relatively unknown. The same customer could not be interviewed twice. The staff also responded to a questionnaire which reviewed this experience of interacting directly with the customer. The information was collected from both these surveys and collated and sent to the Reflect team for further analysis. The OD team used the same questionnaire to conduct FGDs with representative groups of customers–two for each major sub-segment. This first step in the participatory diagnostic exercise generated energy and enthusiasm, particularly because of the positive feedback from customers. The output of the survey itself was interesting and shared during the profiling of the needs of a rural population for financial services.

Organisational Climate Survey

This was based on the organisational climate instrument developed by one of the consultants in her earlier posting as a research officer in NFI. The advantages she had were the suitability for the multi-level, multi-branch structure of Panchim and her familiarity with the whole process.

The organisational climate survey covered the following dimensions:

- Organisational structure.
- Internal communication.
- Resilience and loyalty.
- Managerial processes–goal setting, performance appraisal, reward and punishment, conflict resolution and innovation.
- Team-level processes–interpersonal relationships, customer orientation, trust and support.

The response of the staff to the repositioning of Panchim was useful in assessing the differences between the branches and judging where the OD initiatives had to focus, especially in the behavioural areas.

The instrument was modified a bit and translated into the local language. It seemed to make sense because it engaged all the staff in the process. The climate survey and the FGDs were administered by a team of resource persons involved in the initial diagnosis phase. They were briefed about the process and travelled to various locations where staff and customers had assembled for interactions.

The OD team moved around and administered the questionnaire to staff member groups. About 30 per cent of the staff was covered in this way. They were invited to answer honestly and truthfully about their feelings and thoughts as it was and not report them as it 'ought' to be. The staff members then returned to their locations and administered the forms to their colleagues. The effort was to delink the usual 'official' communication channel for this survey. It ensured good coverage and reliable data too. It was a powerful experience for the respondents because no one had asked such a wide cross-section to state how they felt about their workplace.

Simpler versions of this survey have been found useful when dealing with less hierarchical organisations. Also, it has worked as an FGD framework when studying other organisations.

Presenting Feedback

For these surveys it was made clear to the respondents in the introductory part that individual identity would be kept confidential while the overall picture that comes would be shared with them as part of the change process. Presenting the survey feedback to the staff required some thought and attention. Bar diagrams or pie charts would make no sense to the group. Eventually, the feedback was presented as word pictures–in terms of the thoughts and emotions of the staff member or the customer from a specific segment.

The responses of staff to the repositioning of Panchim were useful in assessing the differences between the branches and judging where the OD initiatives had to focus, especially in the behavioural areas.

Box 7.1 The Survey Results

Word pictures were used for the feedback of the survey results after attempting more 'quantitative' ways like percentages and bar charts. For example, the following profile was translated and shared to bring home the findings of the climate survey.

The views of the Panchim Staff members were:

> They generally involved themselves fully in the work. They recognised the value of NFI's support, but were a bit doubtful about collaboration in the market place. The head office took a long time to take decisions. They would like greater delegation of power. They enjoyed good communication links with each other and informal contacts were strong. They got general information about the developments. Decisions were not communicated so promptly; the grapevine was usually quicker. They enjoyed their work and experienced great autonomy. Superiors generally understood the problems in the field. Some felt that higher standards should have been set for the bank. The resources provided were adequate; training was urgently necessary and relevant. Merit was recognised and nurtured and the approval of bosses was helpful. There was a strong fear of victimisation. Innovations would receive support and rural markets would not be neglected. Computers could solve the problems but would lead to reduction of jobs. There was a need to improve punctuality and discipline. There was awareness of costs and there was scope to be more careful. People came together and volunteered to complete the task. People generally meant what they said and stood by their words.

In their opinion, the bank should urgently find ways to:

- improve customer service,
- reduce interest rates, and
- increase staff number.

A similar method was used for the feedback from customers also.

Shared Diagnosis and Design of Interventions

Some of the information and analysis used through this cycle proved valuable in sharpening the awareness of the staff and generating their enthusiasm for the process. This included:

- Customer feedback in branch specific terms.
- Financial analysis.
- Ranking tool for branches in terms of profitability.

The understanding of the changes in the financial sector when imposed on the organisational diagnosis could support building perspectives for the middle management on the emerging sectoral changes, and engaging with various layers–regulators and policy makers, Panchim board and the microfinance practitioners.

Workshops for Change Agents

Four workshops were organised for the change agents who then took the message from these workshops to the branch-level teams to initiate action in the field. The themes covered in these workshops were at three levels–some inputs on personal effectiveness and managerial and leadership skills for the change agents themselves; strategic thinking on overall vision, structure and innovation, along with conceptual analysis and tools on orientation to customer, product development, loan processing and profit and business planning.

Within the overall design these workshops were facilitated by Zeal and Reflect. The various tools used in this workshop are listed in Table 7.1.

Financial Analysis

The portfolio analysis was in terms of trends in quality and the situation in comparable institutions such as the regional units of NFI, the local co-operative banks and

Table 7.1 Tools and Techniques used in the Workshops—Panchim

Strategy Development	*Team-Building*	*Organisational Mirroring*	*Marketing*	*Knowledge-Building*	*Soft Skills*
Vision Building	Team Roles	Video on Bank	Product Development Activity	Balance Sheet Analysis	Facilitation Skill
Mission Statement	Team Fitness Exercises	Recovery Trip	Role Play for Sales	Performance Score Card	Interpersonal Skills
Goal Setting and Tools for Individual Life Goal Planning		Sharing Experience of Microfinance Organisations			Value Clarification

Reserve Bank of India's (RBI) banking data for the region. For this market share analysis, comparative analyses of loan-recovery performance and portfolio quality were used.

The skills inventory and training needs assessment was based on the existing data and updates by the management. The findings were presented to the management, the board and the change agents. This was useful in aligning the intervention plans and orientation of the selected change agents. They continued to form the basis for the design and delivery of workshops and skill trainings in the second-level change process.

Impact Assessment and Stabilising Change

The impact was assessed against the plans made and NFI found that the process had a positive impact on attitudes, business growth and the bottom line.

In the course of the concluding workshop, it was decided that there was a need for formal working groups to continue the processes initiated. The change agent team presented the details. This was appreciated by the senior managers, and thus work groups were established to continue the work initiated along with building the capabilities of the middle management within Panchim.

Reflections of the Facilitators

(Based on Inputs from Reflect and Zeal)

The Concern-Panchim OD project was a first for Reflect in terms of handling something of this magnitude almost independently. It was also a 'complete' one in terms of the various stages, the planned exit and evaluation. 'It was a project that went well despite the diverse challenges faced.

Box 7.2 P-4 Groups

The idea for the working groups emerged after the review meetings of May 2004. The change agents and managers identified four strategic areas which impacted various activities. The areas of weakness identified were obsolescence of the products, inflexible policy and procedures governing the RRBs, personnel policy, and the gaps in tracking the performance strategically.

It was decided that the P4 Groups would work on these key issues involving members from the change agent group with specific interests and aptitude in the topic. The membership would be rotated every year so that it did not become too much of a burden on a few individuals. It was hoped that these groups would prepare the ground for the emergence of a middle management within the banks. Officials on deputation would not normally become members of these groups. Monthly reports on their deliberations and suggestions would be placed in the structured reviews that would take place in NFI. This would create a direct communication channel from the operational level to the key decision makers. Panchim staff could use this channel effectively to highlight their specific needs from the policy makers. This channel would also help to foster a climate of trust and mutual benefit between Panchim and NFI. It was agreed that these groups would have neither administrative responsibilities nor administrative or financial powers.

Since it happened a while ago, it affords the required distance to reflect on it objectively.'

Why Us?

Usha, the lead consultant from Reflect stated:

> We did not know anyone personally at Concern, a leading international NGO, though we had done some work on training methodologies for their partners in my home state earlier. So the first conversation with Reema (of Concern) over the

> phone was a surprise to me. We recognised the challenges and complexity of the task. But since nothing much seemed to happen immediately, we just went on with life. And then things got going…

The terms of reference itself were well written and clear. The Reflect team was quite excited about the project and preparation soon started.

Building Rapport with Stakeholders

The first meeting between the NFI and the chairman of Panchim took place at NFI's corporate office. Two consultants from Reflect participated and they felt at home in that setting, one of them having worked for NFI earlier, and both having friends there.

The chairman of Panchim and NFI wanted to know how the OD process would help them. The meeting, which took long, gave them enough time to voice their anxieties, get familiar with Reflect, and understand the *one-step-at-a-time* approach that was proposed. A strong alliance between Concern, Reflect, NFI, and Panchim was one of the important outcomes of that meeting.

The discussions about the tools established the norms for working together. After initial attempts to get into the questionnaire design they were quite happy to let it be. The Reflect team too demonstrated readiness to accept suggestions and inputs. The process suggested for data collection–by including the Panchim staff at every stage became an acceptable mode of working. This interaction was very useful in enabling the top leadership to see how the processes around the tasks were the key to change facilitation. The opportunity to voice doubts and fears helped to strengthen the commitment of the chairman to this process.

A Development Agenda

What was the difference in the approach because of a development agenda? The major one was the conviction that the RRBs were very necessary for the well being of the region. One very clearly stated item on the action list was to get the staff to work with SHGs and SHG-promoting organisations as it made good business sense for Panchim. Thus the OD process went with the message of strengthening social banking to attain self sufficiency and did not directly focus on the losses accumulated by the bank. As the process unfolded this aspect was, however, delegated to the background.

Another effort throughout this process was to begin communication and interaction with the regional and national financial and regulatory authorities, and contribute to policy discussions about rural financial systems.

This was perhaps the first time that Panchim staff was challenged to go beyond their habitual complaints and comparisons about salaries and allowances in NFI. They began perceiving their role as agents in social development and gained in confidence.

Building Trust

The Reflect team experienced great freedom and felt free to go one step at a time. Also, there was very little of technical interference in their work, though within the institution there were always people who had their own ideas about how to do things. The external 'experts' would be giving an '*agni pareeksha*', or an 'ordeal by fire', at least in the initial stage.

The staff was open to experience-based learning even though it was not much in use within that system. Usha had been part of the sponsor's system, and this was a strength with the higher Echelons. However, she had to live this down with the Panchim staff, which did not trust NFI. They gradually accepted the authenticity of the stated agenda on behalf of the stakeholders. Explaining the purpose to the Union, the association helped a great deal, which was seen as 'dangerous' by the NFI officials. Even though the chairman was a little apprehensive about these discussions, Reflect was very particular about carrying them out properly. Similarly, the micro labs and role-plays in the initial workshops provided safe platforms for the change agents to express their reservations. Individuals from the representative bodies were also identified as change agents and became the advocates of this process.

There was however some unexpected and rather venomous hostility from the representative of the Central Financial Regulatory Board (CFRB) on the board of Panchim. He seemed to have more reservations about the facilitators than anyone else. This was perhaps a projection of the issues between NFI and the CFRB at the central level and kept surfacing again and again. The consultants opted to remain quiet and let the chairman of Panchim explain the choice of facilitator.

Personal Energy

Usha said:

> As consultants we had many doubts about our ability to influence the flow without becoming 'gurus' or going beyond the consultant threshold. We learnt to invest personal energy in getting at least the key opinion makers to take responsibility for their 'fixed' positions. The first interaction with the change agents proved to be challenging. 'We could empathise with the anger and resentment of the staff.'

But the most surprising aspect was the *naïveté* of the Panchim staff about the larger financial system and where it was headed. The constant competition with NFI for business, salary scales, and perquisites without taking any responsibility for pulling themselves out of the mess they were in, seemed unbelievable. And there were continuing attempts to 'get' something out of even the change process–either from Concern, NFI, or the government. But the consultants had to go beyond such judgements and instead engage with them as they were. The task was to clarify the possibilities and defuse unrealistic expectations.

Partnerships in the OD Process

OD Team

The team at Reflect seemed to build itself–members took charge of the number crunching, survey data, financials, and presentations. They cheerfully handled the data entry and jazzed up PowerPoint presentations. It was a fun-filled stretch in the office, everyone eager to participate and lead the field teams and jointly reflect and build the process gradually. Suneeta from NFI was a great support. She was quite willing to travel and push the managements to keep the schedules despite the preoccupation of their work cycles. The general good cheer made the task of keeping up the pace of work quite easy. The local staff members from Concern who joined in were equally enthusiastic, their participation being high in the initial stage when it was most needed.

'We clearly needed a local partner–we were thinking of approaching a leading NGO in the region when Reema suggested Zeal, a local OD consultant'. Again, it was a very easy partnership–the two consultants developing an instant rapport. They could bond on the basis of the common affiliation with the Indian Society for Applied Behavioural Sciences (ISABS) and other mutual friends.

The local team of Concern helped in the first round of data collection, especially interactions with SHG members. In the later rounds they did not have much of a role. Reema organised the various levels of interactions where these findings had to be presented. She also participated in some of the workshops.

Change Agents

The staff members working as internal change facilitators were the most important part of this OD team. Within the change-agent workshops 'yes but…' syndrome was enacted repeatedly. ('Yes but…' syndrome refers to the pattern of interaction between two people, where one person politely agrees to new ideas but rejects their application or use.)

The important issues to work through were:

- Factions within the Panchim union, association, and the NFI officials on deputation (chairman, GMs, etc.).
- Mistrust and rivalry with NFI in all spheres.
- Introjected sense of inferiority as staff of a loss-making institution.
- Mistrust of the OD process and reluctance to take responsibility.

These issues were addressed through confronting without belittling, handling large group interactions participatively, allowing dissonance and dissent, using the data they generated to show them both positive and negative implications. Despite a general air of lethargy all planned processes were completed as per the design.

Data Analysis and Diagnosis

One thrill that we experienced each time was the clear-cut patterns that the data conveyed.

The challenge was to create a setting where the frontline would examine the patterns and therefore buy into the actions suggested or proposed. Thus presenting of the survey results became very critical. Our effort was to present the picture as it emerged, without adding our opinions, prescriptions, or suggestions.

A narrative style to communicate the survey findings was found useful–creating word pictures of the typical customer from a particular market segment and a profile of the views of the staff members based on the climate survey. It was easily understood and appreciated by everyone.

The gravity of the financial position was presented through a structural analysis of the balance sheets over a period despite apparent shifts. Similarly, objective parameters were developed to identify the top performing and the crisis-ridden branches.

Whatever was presented each time did seem 'new' and very real to the group.

Participative Processes for Data Collection and Diagnosis

Each step in data collection was in itself an emotionally charged experience for the Panchim staff.

They were disgruntled with their status in the banking industry–they wanted to be like other bank employees. This often blinded them to the other advantages, and their own sense of loyalty and commitment to their work. The act of responding to the organisational climate questionnaire gave them an opportunity objectively to assess their organisation, express their opinion and therefore experience relief.

The customer surveys did more to boost their self-esteem than any other process in the whole project. Similarly, recovery drives were a novel experience too. None of them had actually gone and spoken to a customer about the bank. They had never really asked for repayment and they were relieved that many of their fears were unfounded.

The change agent workshops were most useful in affording a 'safe place' to explore their own cliques and subgroups. The bridges built across such divides contributed greatly to strengthening teamwork. Through the series there were opportunities to resolve their differences.

At each stage they would go one level deeper into the diagnosis. The design ensured that work-related issues were discussed among the staff and between the staff and the top management of the banks. The leadership potential available within the change facilitators' group became clear in the course of these workshops.

Building the Collaborative Spirit

The good cheer was kept alive because of the following factors:

- Participants took this seriously.
- Top managers in the bank bought into it.
- There was not much friction among the OD team members.
- Tasks were clear at each stage.
- The workshops were used to bring the resistance to the surface and confront it rather than ignore or overrule it.

Feedback Cycles

To complete the OD process it was very necessary to take some of the key findings into the policy-making levels. This could be done thanks to the micro-finance conference organised by Concern. A paper highlighting the need for more sensitivity to the ground-level constraints in chronic poverty zones was presented and circulated in addition to sharing the OD experience itself.

Relationship between Zeal and Reflect

When Zeal got associated with this intervention it was a tough challenge for them to work on the change plan, both with regard to the context and process. The dilemmas were evident from the very first strategic meeting. A lot of policy-related constraints were discussed. In the second meeting with the key anchors from the NFI, the senior management belittled a previous OD programme and clearly demanded a quantifiable performance-orientation to the OD goal. This was in some sense an uncharted terrain. Despite this, Chandar, the consultant, was quite excited about working with the Reflect team. He could draw strength from the banking experience and significant ISABS experience of the Reflect team as well as his own interest in microfinance and large scale change management initiatives.

Usha recollects:

> The local knowledge and insights available with Zeal about the region–its connects and disconnects, its peculiarities that were spatial as well as psychological, were very useful. Therefore, during the interactions with the chairman, we decided on a calibrated response to organisational changes. During the data collection stage itself some employees were going through a painful un-learning and relearning experience, and our challenge was to make them ready for change in the path of least resistance.

In some sense it was the system-wide initiative, and the resistance to the change came in waves of turbulence and denial that kept surging up all the time. Flexibility built into the design and the available domain knowledge was helpful in structuring a plan to blend the performance/process improvement element in the overall design.

Skill-building Workshops

The four thematic workshops covered most of the issues related to the challenges that were identified. A future focus was brought in using large group facilitation techniques. The perspectives of the entire range of stakeholders, including a few customers, staff, sponsor, and the policy makers of the institution were embedded into the vision-building process. The change agents came together to work on an ideal future living with the current constraints at the organisation level (vision, mission, and goal). They worked on the modification required at the team level to build a high-performance orientation. Transformations at the individual level contributed to sharpen business skills (service level, target understanding and monitoring, managing and conceptualising innovative marketing strategy and products, management of the non-performing assets (bad loans) and so on), role clarity and better management of interpersonal relationships. This was necessary in order to have dual alignment, one at the organisational strategy level, and the other at the values level. The other aspects explored involved tangible issues like infrastructure, technology and process-related issues such as non-financial incentives for staff (in the absence of a formal incentive system) and a participatory monitoring and evaluation system.

The resistance in the system included gender biases against gender, questions about previous work of the facilitators, and so on. To deal with this the OD team strategy was to bring in reality checks and to confront, in a non-threatening manner. The easy technology to capture reality on discreet cameras was used to present a customer service video from a nationalised bank. A real-life recovery trip was critically analysed by participants through role-play.

When the staff members had to simultaneously involve and engage in interactions with customers, with each other, and with neighbourhood branches, a lot of energy was generated within the system, opening up possibilities for collaboration. 'Our challenge was to build on this energy and channel it for constructive purpose,' Usha said.

Most of the time the staff was complaining and blamed the environment for poor customer service. In some cases they were also over-estimating their service quality. Chandar, the consultant from Zeal, spoke to his friends in a larger commercial bank in the coastal district (an area perceived to be superior and better equipped, by the Panchim staff). 'I took permission from this friend to place a video camera in a strategic location to record some interactions with women customers either wanting to borrow or repay,' he said. After masking the bank's identity, a sequence was filmed with the bank's permission. The recording was played to the change agents' group to encourage reflections on what goes wrong with customer service, and as an eye-opener to the real ground situation, irrespective of where the branch is located. The comments on workplace behaviour, processes and empathy–similarity, difference, and other values were all documented. The use of such technology for this kind of mirroring proved to be not only useful but also exciting as well as challenging.

Building a Performance Management Culture

The OD process had to show its commitment to outcomes as a demonstration to the theme of performance-driven culture that was identified as a core issue. Zeal had regular and constant interface with the chairman over the phone or in person. The common vision, a mission and goal at the team level was broken down to individual level through structured exercises. Surprisingly, teams worked through the night to put together a picture as the vision and later on words to it. They kept a pocket book of their individual resolutions with them. It was very clear that the staff was distinctly discomfited by individual level goals. This is where they needed guarantee for environmental level support (from their own top management, sponsors, policy, work place, and teams). The feedback mechanism was introduced to track team-level action plans for performance and work place improvement, product development and related aspects.

Issues were prioritised through a structured exercise in a ballot mode for sequencing. Some structured exercises were used to work on the teams, team role and team-building processes. These methods were chosen from the relevant experience in diverse settings–with a large international NGO, a corporate sector consulting firm and also a private hospital, with varying degrees of success.

Since change stabilisation was the key to the performance management system, a facilitator development module was offered to the identified change agents. They continued to act as facilitators, even after the formal intervention process was over.

Judging Impact

NFI and Panchim acknowledged the impact in terms of improved operations in that year. The documentation is available. We were pleasantly surprised by the outcomes.

The process of involving the Panchim staff in critical decision-making and the transition from supervisory to executive roles had begun. There was cohesion within the staff–to put the interests of the organisation first.

Country Roads ... Pot Holes

Each time the roads were a discovery, the journey was always eventful. Time schedules always went haywire! Some memorable examples:

- Mixed up ticketing and rescheduled flights halfway across the country.
- Flat tyres in the middle of nowhere at 1 a.m., almost doubling the travel time.
- A regular road trip turning into an epic, reminiscent of the story of Moses leading Israel out of Egypt through the Red Sea. The stretch of road we had just driven over suddenly closed by rain and flash floods. Retreat was impossible, the only path – ahead.
- Regular detours due to breaches along major highways.

Larger Forces

'We were left with a feeling of helplessness despite the acknowledged success of the work. With the best of efforts these banks would still find it a challenge to break-even without policy support and major fund infusion (not a likely proposition),' recalled Usha. Though they very much wanted to do something for the staff, the institution and the people they served, yet they knew that little would change in the short run. There seemed hardly a way to reach the policy makers and make them listen!

Perhaps this feeling arose from a close identification with challenges of development in that beautiful yet harsh environment–the men and women–whose simple needs the larger system was ready to ignore. Perhaps it was ambition too–and the political agenda, that was as important as the task of doing a good job of an OD exercise.

While the impact assessment was being carried out, the general elections had just been over. The staff members were sure that they were 'safe' if a certain party/combination was successful. The result was as they had wished, and as predicted by the staff there was a let-up in the pressure to 'do something' about Panchim.

It is only now that there is some further energy on the consolidation exercise proposed nearly two years ago. Hopefully, the lessons of the OD process will now prove useful for these institutions.

Internalising Change—An Assessment

(By the C-POD Reviewer–September 2006)

Motivation for Change

The year 2002 was a watershed year for Panchim. Facing unrelenting pressure to adapt and evolve the need to develop and deliver services in cost-effective ways, and yet stay above the water finally motivated them to seek professional help. At this stage Concern and Reflect stepped in.

The OD group in 2003 identified a number of areas for action, including issues around:

- vision and strategy,
- communication,
- people management,
- product development,
- credit delivery and asset quality and
- operating profits.

Challenges in Organisational Development

The main difficulty was the lack of capacity–both physical and cultural–to take the change initiatives forward. As a consequence, there were plenty of identified issues/initiatives that needed driving forward. The creation of the change management team acted as a catalyst to address the capacity issue. The various barriers to implementing a change management approach were identified, including:

- A diffused focus arising from too many priorities.
- The scale of the organisation and the range of different products.
- Increased competition (for example, own sponsor becoming rival).
- Lack of or poor internal communication.

Role of OD Consultants

The stages in the OD process led to reflection and re-engineering of some of the core processes. The overview of the range of activities enabled the branch-level groups to identify activities and projects that needed to be undertaken. The SWOT analysis of Panchim offered the staff insight on the following aspects:

- Performance management and operational efficiency.
- Identification and sharing of good practices within the organisation.
- Identification of strategies of other organisations and learning from their experience.

The Change Management Team

The OD team recognised the importance of engaging all managers in the improvement process. Some of them functioned specifically as 'change leaders'. They possessed the service and organisational knowledge needed to support the change process and guide others. They did this by working with the consultants to analyse services and processes, identify improvements and implement them.

Besides meeting regularly with the consultants, these 'change leaders' convened as a group to discuss service improvement. The OD team spent a lot of time on a vision exercise and tried to understand core knowledge regarding various processes and culture of the organisation. The approach had helped ensuring that attention was paid to a combination of process and service outcomes. The focus of this work has been on improved benefits for a typical customer and efforts to enlarge the different segments that were seen as less significant earlier. As a result, the 'change leaders' were very enthusiastic about service improvement work and turned advocates for the process improvement.

New Developments after OD Intervention—The Benefits

During my visit to Panchim I was able to meet several change agents and the senior managers, to discuss the impact of the OD process. Some of the changes that seemed to have flown from this OD process were identified as follows:

- Reality check and acceptance of the reality–Awareness about bank performance and sustainability helped the staff to rethink with focus on how to sustain the organisation.
- Provided scope for a distinct vision for their banks.
- The tools and techniques used during the OD process helped them to use and create new process and products.
- Improvement in team work was noticed.
- Communication skills were developed.
- Talented people were identified from within the bank.
- Institutional mechanism for mentoring (the working groups) was developed.

Initially, for about two months, the local consultant often acted as a helpline to the senior management (chairman and GM and some change team and process team leaders).

Process Improvements

Three work groups (out of the P4 groups) have continued to function and their impact is seen in terms of the changes in some core processes. Some of the processes, which have significantly improved, are mentioned here.

Loan Sanction Processes (Scorecard System)

The loan sanction process has improved a lot. While previously it took 45 days to get sanction now the period has come down to three to seven days. The most important reason for this was the new guideline for sanctioning loans and the introduction of a checklist for the loanee. Earlier, most delays were caused by the documentation and query processes. The change has led to business growth–loans have almost doubled within two years. It has also developed the internal capacity to assess, sanction and operate larger loans.

Recovery Process

The experimentation in this regard began with the field visit and role-plays in the change agent workshop. Many innovative processes are now used for recovery of loans. For example, the staff has adopted the *dharna* (sit-in) concept in front of the loanee's house. These efforts are reflected in positive trends in loan recovery and the lowered percentage of non-performing assets (NPAs). The NPA percentage, which was around 24 per cent in 2004, has come down significantly to 18 per cent in 2005 and 13 per cent in 2006.

Letter Issue and Recording Process

The file tracking system that was introduced has dramatically impacted in the productivity of the office. Mails and files now move faster with complete tracking and control over every document. This has helped in removing unnecessary referrals to higher authorities and taken away the irrelevant dependence on the GM. This has of course contributed to building the managerial effectiveness of the middle management layer within Panchim.

Billing System

Simple computerisation has helped consolidate billing. Payments are therefore cleared as early as possible and delays are minimised.

New Product Development

The bank could introduce several new products to meet the emerging needs of their customers identified through the customer contact process. The workgroup on product development continues to be active. They use a structured framework for new product development based on the market need and customer segmentation. The group makes recommendations, which are refined and shaped by a team headed by a GM. The product attributes and costs are detailed and defined and filed with the sponsor bank for approval. These are then taken to the board of Panchim for approval. The new products developed and introduced include:

- Education loan.
- Schemes for the landless (for purchase of land).
- Television for the farmer.
- Personal loan to women.
- Rural (pilgrimage) tourism loan.
- Loan for house development (small furniture).
- Liquid base interest.

These products have a distinct local flavour and no other formal financial institutions offer these options. It is a measure of the effectiveness of this work group that all their recommendations have been accepted by the board and brought into use. This is particularly creditable since new product development is a complex exercise.

Box 7.3 Financial Inclusions

Some of the products introduced meet hitherto unserved requirements of the rural poor.

- Gruha Sova is a personal loan to women.
- Alap–television for farmers reaches where other forms of consumer finance do not reach.
- Gyanlok education loan meets the needs of students.
- Bhumisubihida is a loan for the landless who wish to buy land.

All these have contributed to growth of business as well.

Performance Appraisal

The performance appraisal system now includes a self-appraisal and this opens up space for dialogue and performance counselling.

Conclusion

In the bank employees' view, the roles of the OD practitioners were wide ranging. It included analysing and interpreting data, presenting a clear picture to others of what is happening across the organisation and then establishing priorities for action. Skills in change management, leading and inspiring others and understanding organisational and human behaviour were key learning for employees.

The employees believe that OD practitioners may come from a variety of backgrounds as effectiveness in the role depends more upon individual skills and competencies than professional qualifications. Personal development skills are the key. It is important that the person is able to challenge the existing ways of working and indicate improvements to others.

OD Tools and Techniques

(Based on the Formal Documentation)

Survey Formats

Survey formats, based on the following, can be made available on request. Organisational Climate Survey and SERVQUAL (Zeithaml et al. 1990).

Workshops with Change Agents

There were two intense interactions with the individuals identified as change agents. These workshops were important in that the change agents expressed their reservations, debated implication, and eventually accepted the role of facilitating the change process in Panchim.

Table 7.2 Analysis of Tools and Techniques—Panchim *(Based on the Formal Documentation)*

Activity	*Methodology/Tools*	*Impact/Outcomes*
	Entry	
Discussions with stakeholders (2 days)	Focused group discussions	Alignment within core group on OD approach
	Data Collection and Diagnosis	
Initial climate and customer surveys and FGDs (1 week)	STOC, Servqual variations, customer surveys, FGDs, Organisational Climate Survey, skills inventory and training need analysis	Boosted self esteem and owning up to feelings about the organisation, built shared understanding of the scope of the OD project, led to development of cascade intervention
Data analysis and design of intervention cascade (1 month)	Standard data analysis techniques used such as customer feedback in branch specific terms, financial analysis, ranking tools for branch in terms of profitability	Built perspectives of middle management, objective information on core issues to be addressed in the change process
	Presenting the Diagnosis	
	Presentation to board and NFI	
	Design of Intervention and Selection of Change Agents	
Two Orientation workshops for change agents (2-3 days each)	Feedback from surveys, role of change agents through brainstorming, role plays and extensive group work	Space to express concerns, acceptance of change process, detailed plans for branch level discovery, diagnosis and action planning

(*Table 7.2 continued*)

(*Table 7.2 continued*)

Activity	*Methodology/Tools*	*Impact/Outcomes*
Branch and HO level teams to plan and implement changes.		
	Initiating Action	
Three workshops for change agents at monthly intervals (spread over a period of 3 months)	Field visits, experiential activities, specific tools for monitoring and supervision through tools such as strategy development, team building, organisational mirroring, marketing, credit management and recovery, knowledge building, soft skills	Improvement in core business processes, sensitivity to customer needs
	Assessing Impact	
Review after six months and exit of consultants (1 week)	Measurement of recall of training inputs, analysis of business performance, informal consultations with change agents through questionnaires and focus group discussions	Improvement in credit quality and profitability, achievement of goals identified by change management teams, need for formal groups to continue change processes
	Exit	
Formation of P–4 workgroups to continue the work, share the experience with policy makers and microfinance specialists.		

Table 7.3 Change Agent Orientation Workshop

Goal:	The goal of this exercise was to orient the change agents in various tools and techniques required to be an effective internal change agent
Group:	15-20 members
Process:	(*i*) Introduction to facilitation participative methods (*ii*) Introduction to brainstorming and out of the box thinking (*iii*) Analysis and presentation of the surveys conducted (*iv*) Alignment of ideas regarding process during ODI (*v*) Creation of a self-identity (*vi*) Finalisation of work plan
Tools:	Listening skills, summarising skills, preference ranking, consensus building, brain-storming
Observation:	The mood of the group shifted from one of blaming one another to accepting responsibilities and making attempt to improve the situation. The group was quite enthusiastic to take up various identified tasks and started the process of identifying change agents called "guiding stars"
Outcomes:	Names for the groups (guiding star and *parivartan* coordinator) and plan of action. Volunteers for various tasks in the ODI and their alignment with the task and tracking formats

There were two initial workshops–thereafter the two groups worked together in all subsequent workshops which were to take them deeper into the change process.

Skill-building Workshops

Both standard and context-specific tools have been used in these interventions. The salient elements in the design are:

- Team-building and mirroring exercises to deal with the energy as well as the resistance in the group.

- Developing a clear vision as well as strategy with performance focus (integrating elements of skill, knowledge and attitudinal constructs).
- Relying and confronting the reality with survey feedback.
- Creating space for innovation.

See Tables 7.4, 7.5 and 7.6 for the workshop designs.

Table 7.4 Skill-building Workshop 1—Panchim

Objective:	To introduce a strategic organisational development framework, analyse workplace roles and traits and building skills on portfolio analysis and change facilitation
Time period:	Two and a half days
Participants:	35 members
Sessions:	(*i*) Meet and greet (*ii*) Top five learning in discovery phase: • customer, • collaborator, • self, • competitor and • action plan (*iii*) Portfolio analysis (*iv*) Strategy framework • Visioning • Mission • Goal-setting (*v*) Team fitness and group development (*vi*) Facilitation skills (*vii*) Personality trait and work place roles (*viii*) Action planning

Table 7.5 Skill-building Workshop 2—Panchim

Objective:	To introduce the operational skills like credit management (recovery and NPA), customer service and team roles

(*Table 7.5 continued*)

(*Table 7.5 continued*)

Time period:	Two and a half days
Participants:	32 members
Sessions:	(*i*) *Ghoomta Aina* (rotating mirror) (*ii*) Recap of the last workshop • Vision and mission • Branch action plans • Achievements (*iii*) Credit management in BASIX (*iv*) Video on a bank (*v*) Regulatory issues in credit management (*vi*) Break-even analysis (*vii*) Recovery trip (*viii*) Objective setting and introduction to performance management (*ix*) Team roles (*x*) Action planning

Table 7.6 Skill-building Workshop 3—Panchim

Objective:	To introduce the marketing skills and issues for personal effectives
Time period:	Two and a half days
Participants:	33 members
Sessions:	(*i*) Ballot box (*ii*) Recap of the last workshop (*iii*) Product development framework (*iv*) Marketing of financial services (*v*) Sales role play (*vi*) Presentation on marketing to high net worth customers (*vii*) Johari Window (*viii*) Lecture on highly effective people (*ix*) Value clarification (*x*) Presentation on group development (*xi*) Performance review (*xii*) Experience sharing and action planning

Tools Introduced

At each of the workshops, tools and techniques custom-made for adoption, were presented in the form of activities and experiences. The change agents would then refine it for use within the system. As an example one of the tools is presented here in detail. The performance management tool introduced was based on the *Business Today* framework for ranking banks. The steps are described here.

Objectives

- This is a participatory performance management system where all the managers put together the performance data and see how it reflects on their relative ranks month after month in relation to each other.
- The top management tries to analyse the reasons for the upward and downward movement of the branches and collectively works towards higher performance.
- In the absence of a formal incentive or disincentive this serves as a tool for managing the performance.

Advantages

- The system is participatory, flexible and very simple.
- It is open, transparent and mostly quantitative.
- It allows for the modification of criteria, follows simple algorithm and is easy to manage.
- It uses the current bank MIS to capture data.

Disadvantages

- It is not foolproof.
- It does not provide any security to chronically weak branches; this could be de-motivating.

Techniques

- Enter your key performance data in the spreadsheet.
- Identify criteria to be used (for example, deposit growth, advance growth and so on).
- Discuss and assign weight to each criterion (for example, if you think the deposit is less important than advance then assign a lesser weight to deposit growth and assign a higher weight to advance growth; distribute 100 points to all the criteria chosen).
- Determine how many branches would participate in this ranking. Say ABC has 90 branches. So we have 90 positions. Now run the rank function or sort the individual branches as per the criterion (deposit growth, advance growth and so on).
- Number the ranks. For example, say main branch 'A' has 22nd rank in deposit growth, and then it has a position value of 90–22 = 68. In simple terms it means, the branch has defeated 68 branches to come to the 22nd position.
- Multiply this figure with the weight assigned to the criterion. For example, if this branch has the 22nd rank, then 68 is the rank score, and if we assign 10 points to deposit growth, then we have to have a score for deposit 68 × 10 = 680. Similarly, compute these scores for each criterion. Only this should be reverse for the NPA growth. If the MV65 branch has the highest NPA growth then it should have the lowest rank. That means this has to be sorted in reverse order (descending).
- After a score for each criterion is obtained these scores have to be added to get the total score for each branch.
- Sort the scores and do the rankings for the final total score which is the comparative branch ranking.
- Review and discuss these ranks and learn the story behind the figures. Devise action plans based on the present and past learning. See where you stand next month.

Conclusion

This simple technique serves as a good performance improvement tool as it triggers internal competition, teamwork and the action plans to improve things.

Reference

Zeithaml, V.A., A. Parasuraman, and L.L. Berry. 1990. *Delivering Quality Service; Balancing Customer Perceptions and Expectations.* Free Press.

8

Techniques in Intervention and Design

LALITHA IYER

SOME THEMES THAT EMERGE FROM THE CASE STUDIES

The Common Themes

The common themes that came up in the discussions across these case studies are presented here. There is a need for much deeper and reflective dialogue on all these aspects, and they are set out here to generate further comment and critiquing for knowledge-building in the sector.

Nature of Facilitator-Client System Relationship

This was a theme that recurred through the discussions. The intention or the desire of the facilitator to work in the development space denotes a certain social concern, which motivates the change facilitator. The group was of the view that terms like partnerships or accompaniment better describes the relationship that develops between the facilitator, or external resource person, rather than a consultancy or project. Language of OD presents some problems and it would be preferable to switch to terms like 'institution development' with the involvement of an 'external resource person' or 'facilitator'. Such terminology encompasses many elements important for strengthening work in the field such as OD, HR management, interventions around systems and technology, building CBOs, networking and advocacy.

Balancing the needs of Different Stakeholders

Change facilitators are called upon to work with a variety of stakeholders–funding agency, the leadership of the organisation, the membership/staff, or the community they serve. Very often the consultant is viewed with caution and reserve. The intention of the funding or grant-making organisation is speculated upon. The facilitator is a person who is in contact with all the stakeholders and is considered to have the power to influence the others. The facilitator is expected to be attuned to local and internal culture, and is trusted only if such sensitivity is demonstrated. To meet these often conflicting expectations and demands, the facilitator has to develop ways to communicate authentically and guard against breach of personal boundaries. There is real danger that the facilitator can get pulled into the power and authority dynamics at play.

OD with a Social Change Perspective

Another common assumption seems to be a belief that OD is a 'corporate' fad and therefore an unaffordable luxury for the ordinary NGO. Facilitators have to be able to grasp the development perspective held dear to the organisation, and work in harmony with it. Further, the insights gained from an OD process in the social sector can feed into policy and advocacy work. The change facilitator has to hold these possibilities in mind while designing the OD process. When an OD process is taken up, the organisation is willing to give this process adequate time–unlike the time pressures imposed on consultants in corporate settings.

Measurement/metrics for tracking changes and measuring impact is a more complex issue in the social sector, as the outcome cannot be translated directly into financial terms. It is to be hoped that OD in the social change context will have an impact which is beyond the boundary of the client organisation. Such externalities will further complicate the measurement of impact.

Issues During the Change Process

As in other settings, the facilitator can be restrained to operate safely without challenging status quo. Contributions that seem to have direct and practical application give entry and credibility to the OD process. Nevertheless, barriers come up when the process touches sensitive issues as it is bound to. This is the contradiction that has to be managed. Change, particularly in the social sector, has to be organisation-wide and not just top down. Organisations tend to absorb as much as they want to and ignore the less comfortable parts of the change process, thereby diluting the impact. Facilitation skills thus should presumably lead to greater acceptance.

The possibility of entanglements in the power dynamics within the organisation was discussed. This is a greater danger when the facilitator has a particular 'wish' from this process–such as fulfilling his or her own aspirations for social change. Splitting the consultant role by the client system–forcing a single consultant to do only what is needed for them–or in the case of two consultants, pushing the two apart could be another dynamic.

Exploring Choice of Tools and Techniques

Tools and Techniques

The facilitator should be aware of a variety of ways in which an intervention can be designed and implemented, flexible enough to adapt to the situation at hand. Being alert to unintended consequences at every stage is also useful and can avoid later unpleasantness.

Some of the detailed discussions were around the following points:

- Issues in designing the opening workshop.
- Identifying the hook, sutra or core element of the diagnosis.
- Countering irrational or venomous resistance.

The availability of a colleague to co-facilitate is valuable especially in the initial stages where resistance is high. Based on the situation, it would be useful to include a domain expert in the facilitation team. Often the internal change agent brings in such domain knowledge or perspective.

An intervention is a complex set of activities designed to simultaneously work on several aspects of an organisation for transformation. A comprehensive OD intervention would therefore touch upon all such aspects with varying emphasis at different stages of the change process and the need of the organisation. In the light of the practitioner's reports presented here it is clear that the processes through which a tool is used within the OD cycle as well as its form and content generates such an impact. In this chapter, the methodologies used in the five case studies are seen through a simple framework–to understand the layers at which an intervention can work. Such a dissection will perhaps help the users bring greater craft into the art of OD practice.

Techniques in Intervention Design

Some general observations about intervention design stand out in these case studies.

Variety in Intervention Design

The first noticeable feature is that there is no readymade template or model for designing an intervention. The practitioners have made little use of standard textbook tools. They have instead woven in some 'standard fare' (for example, Johari window) into their workshops, often presenting the idea or concept very differently.

Box 8.1 Johari Window—*avatars*

In the Panchim case study, the concept of Johari window was used to strengthen individual capacity to give and receive feedback. It was used to prepare change facilitators to work with inter-branch teams to influence communication norms, especially within peer groups. The change facilitators shared this with the inter-branch teams they worked with. In terms of the VanSant classification this may be seen as an intervention to strengthen the human resources of the institution.

In Triveni, an intervention for institutional sustainability, enhancing the systems capacity to learn from the environment, the same concept was used differently. It was used to enable the participants to see individual as well as systemic blind spots. It was used in all the workshops they organised.

This is to illustrate how the very commonly used tools and ideas take on meaning and significance in the way they are positioned within an intervention.

Johari Window is a cognitive psychological tool created by Joseph Luft and Harry Ingham in 1955 in the United States. This used to help people better understand their interpersonal communication and relationships.

The Opening Workshop

The design of the opening workshop is very significant. The duration seems to range between three and six days. It combines some personal reflection, experiencing the external realities and identifying directions for the future. The willingness to set aside the required time and commit a reasonably important cross-section of the organisation is perhaps a signal that the system is eager to change. The processes used are typically those appropriate for large scale interactive (LSI) sessions.

Data Collection and Feedback

Data collection often happens in and from the workshop itself. The data generated by the participants themselves, and the consultants' observations and intuitive abilities are offered to the group for analysis and diagnosis. The device of including resource persons or guest speakers to bring in perspectives from different settings (like academics and business and political systems), has been used in one case study. Very often more formal assessments and reports are available for the consultant to gain an initial understanding. The consultants seem to have placed much importance on visiting the 'field' in all the case studies. It has been important for them to develop a fair understanding of the ground realities as a part of the diagnostic phase used in two cases. Survey has been used as a technique at this stage in one of the case studies. Here too, the process of administering the survey becomes an intervention in itself.

Learning Events

The learning events seem to integrate various elements such as:

- Personal and interpersonal skills like communication, listening and facilitation–usually addressed through experiential activities;
- Group level and managerial processes in organisations–like leadership, teamwork and decision-making;
- Task related inputs focussing on feedback mirroring and reviewing to improve core service processes and activities;
- Changes in systems with a good background on the need for change and special aspects to be noted; and
- Strategic analysis at self-level–personal goals, vision or values, team level–inventories like team role or team fitness and organisational level–shared vision, mission and values.

The specific mix in a learning event would depend on the group and its role, the stage in the OD process, and the needs identified overall. The assessment of the levels of resistance to change prompts a design with appropriate open spaces to voice disagreement or doubt. These events can be clearly differentiated from training programmes that are specific to the learning needs of a specific subgroup in the organisation, like an induction programme or MDP.

Development Centres

Development Centres have been used in one intervention to methodically identify the distinguishing competencies for the organisation and assessing the group of potential leaders to provide them feedback and coaching to meet organisational expectations. Since this is a specialised technique, experts in this methodology were invited to take up the work.

Improvements in Internal Systems

There are many examples of work around internal systems in these five reports. The distinguishing feature is that they have either been developed by internal experts, or sourced from the market. In Ekta the 360-degree feedback and performance appraisal system was provided by a leading expert in this area. Alternatively, some tools have been designed especially to suit the situation. Some systems have been introduced by the consultants themselves. Profit planning, product development and credit processing tools for Panchim were offered by Zeal. These were adapted for use by the management of Panchim. '*Koodam*' was a process intervention used in Triveni. It is an effective way for open and frank dialogue within a very rigid system without threatening the overall political system but has the power to gradually transform it.

Given this variety and range of tools and techniques used in the interventions, it becomes important to seek a larger picture to understand how to choose or drop a particular element. A framework developed to assess institutional capacities of non-profits is used to attempt such an analysis.

Common Categories of Institutional Capacity

Prof. Jerry VanSant of Duke University discusses the common elements of institutional capacity in NGOs, which fall into three major clusters. OD interventions can therefore be understood in terms of the intended (and actual) effect in supporting capacity improvements through facilitating changes in these elements (VanSant 2000).

Institutional sustainability incorporates more forward-looking attributes such as organisational autonomy, leadership and learning capacity that in turn help ensure sustainability and self-reliance in the future.

Table 8.1 Elements of Institutional Capacity

Institutional Sustainability	*Institutional Resources*	*Institutional Performance*
Leadership	Human resources	Programme results
Organisational learning	Management systems and practices	Application of technical knowledge
Organisational autonomy	Legal structure and governance	Networking and external relations
	Financial resources	Constituency empowerment

Source: VanSant (2000).

Institutional resources represent the attributes an organisation possesses or controls and consists of its basic legal structure, assured access to human, financial, technical and other resources and its management systems and structure, including performance management systems.

Institutional performance measures an institution's programme, services or other impacts, to show how effectively it employs its institutional and technical resources. For development organisations, external relations and the empowerment of civil society are frequently key intended outcomes. Institutional performance assesses both efficiency and effectiveness at a point in time.

Interventions to Strengthen Institutional Sustainability

OD may be seen as a planned process to improve the sustainability of an institution. The case studies here provide examples of interventions that focus on these aspects.

Leadership

Chaturya is an example of an intervention focussed entirely on leadership development and experimentation with a collective leadership model. In Ekta, the interventions with the top leadership enabled a transition that gave greater autonomy to people down the line. In Triveni, the engineers in the change management groups (CMGs) were able to go beyond technical efficiency, towards effectiveness in a particular social context, thereby strengthening their managerial and leadership capabilities. In Prakruti, the effort was to recognise and build leadership qualities among women in the organisation, and in the community. In Panchim, the change facilitators, who saw themselves as mere supervisors, began to recognise their leadership abilities. Work at the level of individuals within an organisation to tap their leadership potential is therefore a crucial element in any change process. It opens up possibilities of creativity and transformation, especially when fitted into other elements of institutional change. The work requires good quality human process facilitation because it often challenges existing hierarchies of power and authority. Norms of communication are reshaped with flows of exchange being opened up in many new directions. The energy unleashed has to be channelised for functional adaptation within the organisation.

Organisational Learning

Leadership development and personal growth interventions have to take the next step, of linking up to the long-term needs within the organisation, in order to make an impact. Interventions that provoke reflection on the core purpose of an organisation, especially in a changing external context, can help the internal leadership to come together on their core task. The writers in these case studies describe how they intervened to facilitate such organisational learning processes.

The opening workshop has been used in four case studies to get the organisations to reflect on the current reality and the emerging needs, and build a shared vision for the future. The Ekta 2010 workshops and the four workshops leading to the Triveni Declaration show how a mix of different processes–personal, interpersonal and large system level have to be combined to move the organisation towards a shared vision. The external realities also have to be brought home in a convincing manner to mobilise energies for change within the organisation. Inputs from external experts and other stakeholders are again useful in challenging the status quo. The gap between what is stated (as overall goal or perspective), and what is actually practiced, is also brought out in these workshops. These opportunities created for organisational learning are therefore valuable in the way they enable transformations from the individual to the organisational level to bring about alignment with the strategic purpose.

One important item in organisational learning has been the 'change sutra' or 'hook' of the core beliefs, which actually shape the organisation's strategy. The change facilitators are usually groping for this in the initial diagnostic phase and it gradually emerges from the data and the process. This is the process of making explicit some of the limiting assumptions and mental models. Once such an assumption is tested against reality, it is possible to proceed further and create new pathways into the future. Sometimes the learning from some other unrelated situation also helps in unravelling the change sutra–as the notion of ecology and its relationship to gender did in Prakruti.

Organisational Autonomy

An important aspect for sustainability is the capacity that an organisation gains to exercise its own choice within the given operating environment. This issue too gets clarified in a strategic thinking exercise. The sense of helplessness that people within an organisation sometimes experience gets challenged in such a process.

The issue has been addressed in two ways. Explorations and dialogue with external stakeholders has helped the organisation to generate a larger pool of options so that choosing is a reality. At another level creating space for individuals within the organisation like the internal change agents to experiment and innovate, has opened up opportunities for individuals to take charge and unleash the potential for transformation.

Another aspect of autonomy would be the ability developed in an organisation to continuously learn and innovate even without the prodding of a change facilitator or consultant. The P4 groups in Panchim and the CMGs in Triveni are examples of informal or semi-formal structures created to continue the changes initiated during the change process. These have proven to be valuable in sustaining the processes initiated during the OD effort.

Interventions for Institutional Resource Development

All the case studies have included interventions to strengthen the institutional resources, which are summarised here.

Human Resources

OD projects by definition involve steps to strengthen the human resources. The interventions described in these case studies have been described here.

Prakruti, with its focus on gender, had gender sensitisation workshops and initiatives to build capacities of the women staff members. The staff members were also exposed to workshops on facilitation skills, team development and sensitisation to social issues.

The Ekta process included several measures to strengthen the human resources such as:

- Development centres to assess competencies and plan for their development.
- Skill-building workshops based on learning needs identified with elements of personal growth and leadership development.
- Recruitment and retention strategies for staff, induction processes, defining HR policies, rationalising compensation and benefits, 360-degree feedback systems, and so on.

Triveni sought to build the capacity of the government engineers to deal with social concerns. Similarly, Panchim tried to build the capacity of the Panchim staff to deal effectively with their customers, particularly self-help groups (SHGs). Chaturya tried to develop the leadership potential available within the organisation.

Management Systems and Practices

The core issue in Triveni was strengthening the management systems. Similarly, many management practices were studied and strengthened in Panchim. Tackling gender role stereotyping and strengthening the role of women staff in programme management was an aspect of intervention in Prakruti. In Ekta, the management development programmes were set in the context of the organisation and the outcomes went to strengthen their managerial systems.

Legal and Governance Aspects

The governance structure of Ekta was strengthened throughout the four years of the intervention with clarification of boundaries and role differentiation. There were efforts to change the styles of interaction within the EC and the CMG, to foster innovation and change. In all the other case studies, the governance structure of the organisation was relatively untouched. However, issues of good governance and stakeholder involvement were part of the work.

The board (or similar apex authority) was the primary advocate for the OD efforts in all these cases, providing it legitimacy and acting on the necessary changes. In Triveni, the project director could successfully negotiate for enough room in a highly structured bureaucratic setting, and his superior authority supported the project consistently. In Panchim, an effort was made to raise issues on regulation and pricing policies in rural banking on the basis of the feedback generated. The peril of ignoring the governance structure is highlighted in Chaturya. Prakruti was invited to address the questions of women being marginalised in the watershed programme, and was able to shift the attention both inward and outward.

Financial Resources

Financial viability was a major concern in the Panchim project. The project sponsors were happy with the improved financial performance as a result of the OD process. In Triveni also, the cost effectiveness of an intervention of this nature, in impacting project cost and efficiency was highlighted. This issue was, however, not in the forefront in the other cases.

Interventions to Strengthen Institutional Performance

The OD consultant is usually not a domain expert and does not directly intervene in the programmatic aspects. However the participants in the OD chain with the required domain knowledge work on the institutional performance related issues.

Programme Results

In Ekta, the seven major themes of work were identified and the work processes reviewed and strengthened. Similarly, in Panchim, the workgroups at various levels tracked workplace issues within the overall framework generated by the diagnosis. The monthly accompaniment visits in Prakruti were aimed at studying the work in the field to improve the gender balance in the field programmes. The change management groups set up in Triveni carried out projects to improve service delivery.

Application of Technical Knowledge

Two aspects recur with regard to the consultant's role in building, or using technical knowledge. One is the contribution of internal change facilitators and the other is the question of the level of domain knowledge needed in such works. In these case studies the internal change agents have played a major role in making improvements in the field performance, while consultants have called in domain experts when needed. Even when the consultant has domain knowledge, the challenge is to use it in such a way that it frees rather than controls the internal talent.

Networking, External Relations and Constituency Development

The OD process has sought to redefine external relations, especially with the stakeholders who were not so well represented earlier. In the case of Prakruti the focus is on the constituency of women, both within and outside the organisation. In Triveni it is the water user especially from the marginalised sections. In Ekta, the development of CBOs is a major feature of the effort, which was strengthened in the process. In Panchim and Chaturya, the user communities were not brought into the process in this manner.

Networking with other organisations was not a prominent theme in any of these case studies.

Balanced Inputs for Planned Transformation

It is clear that some processes are deemed 'essential' OD inputs such as strategic planning and training and capacity-building for staff. The impact of these activities can be sharper if the design pays adequate attention to the tough but important elements like governance issues and autonomy for and within the organisation. On the whole, the design based on sustainability factors and focussing on resource development within the organisation should create opportunities for performance-related initiatives to improve the situation even further.

Need for OD Practice in Social Sector

The participants were keen to set up ways to continue to work together. There is a clear recognition that consultants with adequate awareness of social perspectives are urgently required, particularly to work with large NGOs and government projects.

The initiative and support from SRTT has fostered the growth of a community of practitioners who have benefited from the availability of a common space to share their concerns. The way forward now seems to be:

- To enlarge the scope by use of the term institution building rather than organisational development.
- To publish the material generated through workshops and conferences.

- To continue the documentation efforts along the lines discussed in the conference.
- To support more such exploratory workshops across sub-sectors and around a specific theme.
- To use the knowledge gained to shape grant-making policies and procedures.

Themes for Further Documentation

Some clear themes for documentation have emerged as a natural sequel to this collection and they are:

- Experiences of organisations in absorbing change through long-term HR work on leadership development, social entrepreneurship, HR systems for building scale and reach, technology absorption, decentralisation, and so on.
- Assessment of the direct impact of OD processes and their contribution to developmental outcomes and policy change.
- Addressing governance and institutional development issues, particularly in engaging the political, bureaucratic, judicial, financial and other large systems.
- Facilitating organisational change through systems improvement and quality initiatives.

Conclusion

The purpose in sharing this is to highlight the state of OD practice particularly in the social development arena. The contributions of the participants in the conference and their deep involvement in the discussions made it a memorable occasion. This collection is published in the hope that it would stimulate others to come forward and document their stories too.

Reference

VanSant, J. 2000. 'A Composite Framework for Assessing the Capacity of Development Organizations'. Prepared for USAID. Available online at http://www.g-rap.org/docs/ICB/USAid%202000%20capacity%20assessment.pdf. Downloaded on 24 June 2008.

About the Editors and Contributors

C-POD Team

Lalitha Iyer is a professional member of the Indian Society for Applied Behavioural Sciences (ISABS). She is an institutional development consultant and facilitator. Her book *The Strategic Business Spiral* (2001. New Delhi: Sage [Imprint: Response]) offers a model for strategic change. She has experience of over two decades in the State Bank of India and was a member of faculty at State Bank Staff College, Begumpet. She was principal of Vidyaranya, a leading school in Hyderabad, for a few years and is now with Think-Soft Consultants, Hyderabad. She is currently a director in Bharatiya Samruddhi Financial Services Ltd (Basix) and remains closely associated with Ananda Bharathi, Anveshi, the Henry Martin Institute and Yugantar.

Shaibal Guharoy is a freelance writer and editor based in Hyderabad. He has been writing since 2002 for various companies and advertising agencies. He has also written a few short stories, a couple of which have been published in Anthologies.

Mamta Uppudi is a researcher and consultant working on development and organisational issues. She is a postgraduate in HRD sciences from the Madras University and is currently working on the theme of counselling support for children in difficult circumstances.

Conference Facilitators (C-POD II)

Rolf Lynton, a PhD in Policy Science, has a long career in institution building and development in India and elsewhere. Beginning with his own World War II experience of factory work and management (*Incentives and Management in British Industry,* 1949, London: Routledge and Kegan Paul) he has authored and co-authored several papers, chapters and books. Best known in several editions in the USA and in India and Indonesia is the two-volume *Training for Organisational Transformation* with Udai Pareek (2000. Sage: New Delhi), and the most personal is *Social Science in Actual Practice* (1998. Sage: New Delhi).

H. Ronken Lynton was born and brought up in Minnesota, with links to the Scandinavian community there. She broke with the family tradition and went off to Radcliffe to study. After working in Washington during World War II, she became the third woman to be appointed to the Harvard Business School faculty and was one of the pioneers in developing case writing as a learning methodology. In 1953, Rolf Lynton came to her department on a fellowship, and in 1955 they were married and set out for Asia. Of the past fifty years, besides travelling in Asia they have spent more than twenty years in India, five in Indonesia, and one in Botswana. She has published management books, as well as three biographies of leading Indian figures. An accomplished novelist, she has just published her novel set in America.

Contributors and Reviewers

Ganesh Anantharaman holds an MPhil in Political Science and began his career as a lecturer in Mumbai. He has since worked both in industry and the development sector in the HR area. He moved into Applied Behavioural Sciences, getting accredited to Indian Society for Applied Behavioural Sciences (ISABS) as a professional member. He is now a training and OD consultant with Organizations and Alternatives, Bangalore. He has a special interest in value clarification laboratories and in the Group Relations Conference methodology, and has worked as a staff member in the first ever online GRC. He is passionate about music and his book on popular music is expected shortly.

Pratap J. Das is based in XIM Bhubaneshwar with a special interest in understanding and documenting service process and reengineering core business processes. His other interests are OD and process documentation.

Lalitha Iyer

A. J. James is a specialist in evaluation monitoring and has founded Pragmatix in Gurgaon, which specialises in assessing impact and social change. His review was used in one of the cases studies.

Shirish Joshi has worked in both the public and private sectors after doing his MMS from Jamnalal Bajaj Institute, Mumbai. He was head of HR and member of the executive council for Thermax Group of Companies. Apart from revamping the compensation policy and strategy, he was known for envisaging compensation as an OD intervention in Thermax. This exposure offered him an intimate understanding of changes in the business and HR processes in some of the largest companies in India. He was also a member of CII's National HRD Committee. He is a HR, OD consultant to many companies and non-profit organisations. He is keenly interested in the development of local institutions and community-based organisations. He is a visiting faculty at XLRI, Jamshedpur.

Anuradha Prasad is the executive director of Human and Institutional Development (HID) Forum, Bangalore. Her basic degree is in Home Science, after which she moved to Agricultural Extension for her MSc and PhD degrees. Her interest in agricultural labour issues led her to work for the National Labour Institute for some time. She then worked with Swiss Agency for Development and Cooperation (SDC) for several years. She is currently the Dean, Professional Development of Indian Society for Applied Behavioural Sciences (ISABS), and is invited as staff member for Group Relations Conferences (GRC) across the world. She had been interested in Jungian analysis and trained a variety of Applied Behavioural Sciences methodologies. She is on the board of Kutch Mahila Vikas Kendra and several other important NGOs.

Pradip Prabhu is currently the national convenor of the National Campaign for Tribal Self Rule and senior fellow, National Institute of Rural Development, Hyderabad. He is also part of the Centre for Law, Policy and Human Rights Studies, Chennai. He is a legal activist of the Kashtakari Sangathana at Dahanu. He is also the convenor of the National Front for Tribal Self Rule that has spearheaded the struggle for self governance and has played a major role in the formulation and passage of Panchayat Extension of Scheduled Areas Act.

K.S.S. Rau joined the State Bank of India (SBI), Ahmedabad as a Probationary Officer in 1972 after his post graduation in English Literature. Besides the range assignments in banking operations, Mr Rau specialised in Training and Development with a special interest in Applied Behavioural Sciences and Marketing. He left SBI to head the HR function in the South Indian Bank Ltd, Trissur. He is currently a freelance OD and training consultant based in Hyderabad.

Haritha Sarma has been working in the development sector for over ten years. He began his career as a hydrogeologist and worked in the area of Natural Resource Management for five years. He is now with HID Forum, Bangalore as a programme executive. He is an experienced gender trainer and accompanies organisational change initiatives in many groups and organisations in Karnataka and Andhra Pradesh.

V. Suresh, a consultant in change management and institutional transformation, has been the external consultant involved with the democratisation project in the Tamil Nadu water utility. For the last ten years he has been involved in good governance initiatives in large government utilities with state-level institutions covering school education, health and social welfare departments, and Government of Nagaland on a UNICEF-supported 'Good Governance in Nagaland' project. Additionally, he is the general secretary of the Tamil Nadu and Pondicherry state units of a national level human rights organisation, People's Union for Civil Liberties (PUCL). He is also part of the Centre for Law, Policy and Human Rights Studies, Chennai.

Roopantaran—An Initiative of the Sir Rata Tata Trust

The Sir Ratan Tata Trust (SRTT) (www.srtt.org) is one of the oldest philanthropic institutions in India and offers institutional grants in areas of Rural Livelihoods and Communities, Education, Health, Art and Culture and Enhancing Civil Society and Governance.

SRTT initiated Roopantaran under its civil society and governance theme to build vibrant non-profit organisations through Human Resource Development (HRD), Organisation Development (OD) and Institution Building

(IB) processes. This initiative arises from the basic belief that strengthening organisations is a meaningful contribution to the sector. Roopantaran focuses on building knowledge and human resources for OD for the non-profit sector including: (*a*) support to select non-profit organisations with proven programmatic track records in undertaking OD interventions; (*b*) create a community of OD practitioners to share their experiences in supporting non-profit organisations resulting in documentation of best practices and tools; and (*c*) create a larger pool of professionals drawn from various disciplines/fields of development action.

A Community of Practitioners in Organisation Development (C-POD) was formed under Roopantaran to share experiences of institutional change facilitation and document the challenges on the ground.

Index

access to common resources
process-based reform and, 12
accompaniment process, 93

change and reworking identity, 11
change management group (CMG)
formation, in Triveni, 122–24, 199
projects identified by, 123–24
Chaturya, 200–01
collective leadership, 76–78, 82
collective leadership intervention, 62–63
consultants
clarity on client, 74
exit of, 72
linkages with all stakeholders, 75
process of entry, 73–74
reflections of, 73–75
report to CEO and SMT, 71–72
setting boundaries to, 75
context and institutions involved, 60–61
impact assessment of OD process, 76–78
OD process and event structure, 62–72
OD tools and techniques, 78–83
organisational structure of, 62
workshops, 63–70, 78, 81–83
on collective leadership for SMT, 65–68, 78, 81–83
consultative process for resolution of dilemma, 82
dilemma on methodology, 81
with extended management team, 68–70, 83
external resource person in, 82–83
objectives, 63, 65, 69
outcomes, 64–65, 67–68, 70
processes in, 64, 66–67, 69–70
transferring ownership to SMT members, 83
collective leadership
in Chaturya, 76–78, 82
intervention in Chaturya, 62–63
in small organisation, 11–12
common resources, democratisation of access to, 12
community based organisations (CBOs), 29
community participation, in programme choices, 11
consultant-client relationship, 13–14
C-POD (Community for Practitioners in Organisation Development)
frameworks for documentation, 13–17

further agenda for, 203
themes for further documentation, 205–06
C-Pod II, 18–21

Development Centres (DCs), and Ekta, 31–32, 38, 47, 56–57, 193

Ekta Development Research Foundation (Ekta), 22–59, 196, 198–99, 201, 202–03
assessment, 44–51
changes in key processes, 45–46
communication styles, 49–50
OD process, 46
points of disagreement, 47–48
source of discord, 49
campus recruitment and induction processes, 32–33
CMG meeting on OD process, 27, 198, 200
communication styles in, 49–50
context and institutions involved, 22–24
360-degree feedback and performance appraisal, 32, 196, 201
Development Centres (DCs), 31–32, 38, 47, 56–57, 195
EC and CMG role and functions, 28–30, 47
Ekta 2010 meeting, 25–27, 51–52, 55–56, 199
facilitator reflections, 35–44
change *sutra*, 37–39
clarity and structure, 40–41
closure, 42–43
freedom within constraints, 40
influencing culture, 41
insider and outsider role, 42
mental models redefining, 39
multiple roles, 41–42
scientific orientation, 38
HR policy manual, 30–31
flexibility in employment, 30
remuneration issue, 31
intervention cycle at, 28
interventions impact, 33–34
issues of concern for, 23
management development programmes (MDPs), 33, 47, 57–59
OD event structure, 24–35
OD initiatives, 33–34
OD tools and techniques, 52, 55–59
analysis, 53–54
Development Centres, 56–57
Ekta 2010 meeting, 51–52, 55–56
MDPs, 57–59
organisational structure, 24–25
success factors, 27
SWOT, 55
Ekta 2010 meeting, 25–27, 51–52, 55–56, 199
Emergent Cyclical Levels of Existence Theory, 55
Existential Universe Mapper (EUM), 57

Force Field Analysis, Triveni, 143–44

gender
concept in intervention, 111
mainstreaming intervention, 85–99

role definition, 12
sensitive organisation profile, 112–13

institutional
performance and resources, 195
sustainability, 195–98
Institutional Transformation Group (ITG), 116
intervention and design
for institutional resource development, 200–02
financial resources, 200
human resources, 198–99
legal and governance aspects, 199–200
management systems and practices, 199
to strengthen institutional sustainability, 195–98
leadership, 195–96
organisational autonomy, 197–98
organisational learning, 196–97
to strengthen institution performance, 200–02
constituency development, 201–02
inputs for planned transformation, 202
networking and external relations, 201–02
programme results, 201
technical knowledge application, 201
techniques in
data collection and feedback, 192
Development Centres, 193
improvements in internal systems, 194
institutional capacity elements, 194–95
Johari window, 191
learning events, 192–93
opening workshop, 192
variety in intervention design, 191
themes, 187–89
change process, 189
facilitator-client system relationship, 187–98
needs of stakeholders, 198
OD with social change perspective, 188–89
tools and techniques choice, 190–202
for Triveni, 124–26
intervention cycle, for Triveni, 118
intervention process, gender concept in, 85–97, 111

Johari Window adoption, Triveni, 142–43, 191

Koodam, Triveni, 119–20, 142, 194

large scale interactive process (LSIP) model, 26, 194

management development programmes (MDPs), and Ekta, 33, 57–59, 195
mid-course process review, 14

OD tools and techniques
for Chaturya, 79–80
for Ekta, 51–59
in intervention and design, 192–97

for Panchim, 179–87
for Prakruti, 107–10
for Triveni, 140–45
organisational structure
of Chaturya, 62
of Ekta, 24–25
of Prakruti, 85–86
of Triveni, 117
organisation development (OD) process
academic viewpoint, 10
in Chaturya, 62–72
completion of programme and exit, 7
consultancy task definition, 3–4
contact making, 2–3
data collection, 5
diagnosis and design of interventions, 5–6
in Ekta, 22–59
entry stage, 8
and event structure
of Chaturya, 62–72
of Ekta, 24–34
in Panchim, 147–58
for Triveni, 117–29
initiating action, 6–7
persistent difficulties, 8–9
in Prakruti, 102–04
selection of project, 3
stages of, 2
terms of reference, 3–4
themes for interventions, 4
in Triveni, 117–29
view of client systems, 9
organisation development (OD) programmes framework, 15–17

Panchim OD process, 196, 198, 200, 201–04
assessment, 172–78
benefits of OD intervention, 174–75
billing system, 176
challenges in OD, 172–73
change management team, 173–74
financial inclusion through product range, 177
letter issue and recording process, 176
loan sanction process, 175
motivation for change, 172
new product development, 176–77
OD consultants role, 173
performance appraisal, 177
process improvements, 175
recovery process, 175–76
change agent selection and orientation, 149–50, 156
and event structure, 147–58
facilitators reflections, 158–72
building rapport with stakeholders, 160
building trust, 161–62
development agenda, 161
partnerships in OD process, 163–72
personal energy, 162–63
P-4 groups, 159
financial analysis, 156, 158
impact assessment and stabilising change, 158
objectives, 145–47
organisational structure of Panchim, 150
partnerships in, 163–72
change-agent, 164
collaborative spirit building, 166

data analysis and diagnosis, 165
data collection and diagnosis, 165–66
feedback cycles, 166–67
judging impact, 170
OD team, 163–64
performance management culture, 169–70
skill-building workshops, 168–69
stakeholders in, 148
steps involved in
change agents workshop, 156–57
customer feedback, 152–53
description of, 151–56
diagnostic survey elements, 151–52
Focus Group Discussions (FGDs), 152
interventions design, 156
organisational climate survey, 153–54
presenting feedback, 154
shared diagnosis, 156
survey results, 155
surveys for, 148–49
tools and techniques, 178–86
analysis, 179–81
change agent orientation workshop, 181
objectives and advantages, 184
skill-building workshops, 182–83
survey formats, 178
workshop designs, 182–83
workshops with change agents, 178
workshops on critical themes, 150–51
Prakruti, 198, 200–02
gender mainstreaming intervention, 86–99
capacity-building for women staff, 93
design of interventions, 89–91
entry process, 87
facilitation skills enhancement, 94
monthly accompaniment visits, 93
outcomes, 95–96
people and organisational processes, 91–92
perspective building on gender, 92, 94
reflections and lessons learnt, 96–99
review meetings, 94
terms of reference, 88
training tools on gender, 94
understanding of organisation, 89
OD method
assessment, 100–108
attitude towards women staff members, 106
changes in perceptions in village, 105–06
consulting organisation, 101
contracting process, 101
gender mainstreaming, 100–101
impact on structures, systems and processes, 105
reviewer's observations, 107–08
Steering Committee, 105
triggers for process, 100

OD process
accompaniment process, 102
capacity-building for women staff, 104
documentation, 104–05
feedback from village, 103–04
sensitisation of field staff, 103
steps in, 102–05
OD tools and techniques, 108–10
organisation, 85–86
strategy and approach, 86

regional rural banks (RRBs), 145–46, *see also* Panchim
reworking identity, of change and gender, 12
rural financial institution, viability through social perspectives, 13

scheduled activities review, 14–15
small organisation, collective leadership in, 11
social banking, 146–47
social sector, organisational change and institution building in, 1–9

technically oriented programme, in social perspectives, 11
Total Community Water Management project, 139
Triveni, 196, 198–203
assessment of change, 134–38
better targeting, 136
community contribution, 135
conservation and recharge, 137–38
cost-effective solutions, 136
cost reduction, 135
institutional building, 137
planning, 136
savings, 136
context and institutions involved, 114–17
facilitators reflections, 129–31
at entry stage, 129
negotiation with project management, 131
OD introduction to department, 130–31
resource persons background, 130
lessons for managers, 138–39
OD process and event structure, 117–29
assumptions, 126
basic construct, 127–28
change management group (CMG) formation, 122–24, 141
change projects, 123
initial training interventions, 118–19
institutional change, 125–26
integrating learning through field visits, 128
intervention cycle, 118
intervention design, 124–26
Koodam, 119–20, 128, 142
mind-sets, 124–25
process to explore organisation, 119–20
projects identified by CMG, 123
shared vision, 120–21
training design, 127
OD tools and techniques, 139–44
Force Field Analysis, 143–44

Johari Window adoption, 142–43
Koodam, 142
learning from critiquing existing schemes, 144
understanding water crisis, 139, 142
organisational structure, 117
partnership for interventions, 131–34
consolidating change, 133
project director role, 134
resistance from within organisation, 132–33
Triveni Declaration, 120

village water and sanitation committees (VWSCs), 137, 141

women's thrift and self-help movement, 146